OF

D1439650

COUNTRYSIDE BOOKS
3 Catherine Road
Newbury, Berkshire

To view our complete range of books,
please visit us at
www.countrysidebooks.co.uk

ISBN 1 85306 768 7

For my good friends, Bert and Anita Bruffell

Produced through MRM Associates Ltd., Reading
Typeset by Mac Style Ltd, Scarborough, N. Yorkshire
Printed by J. W. Arrowsmith Ltd., Bristol

Contents

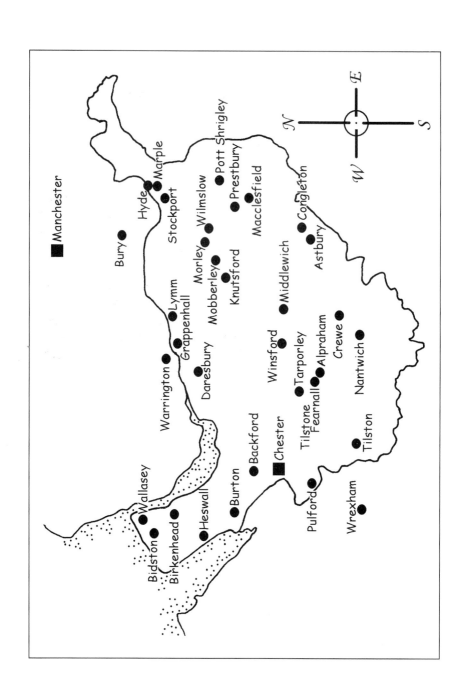

Introductory Note

A book entitled *Cheshire Tales of Mystery & Murder* calls for little in the way of an introduction: the title is almost self-explanatory. Almost, but not quite. In the interests of clarification, it is necessary to state that, for the purposes of this book, the term 'Cheshire' will be used to denote the historic county. That is, the area discussed in the authoritative *The Victoria History of the County of Chester* (Oxford University Press for the University of London, 1987) – the once-proud County Palatine – not the present administrative county, created by the Local Government Act of 1974, which is markedly different. See map opposite.

ACKNOWLEDGEMENTS

I gratefully acknowlege my debt to the following people, without whose help I could not have written this book: those retired police officers who helped me in their private capacities, but wish to remain anonymous; Rev Canon David Ashworth, Vicar of Prestbury; Ian Boumphrey, local historian and writer, for help with the illustrations; Rev David Felix, Vicar of Daresbury; Pam Hall, Secretary, Frodsham Local History Society; Mike McManus, Chairman, Supernatural Encounters Association; Audrey Meecham, churchwarden, St Christopher's church, Pott Shrigley; Paul Mitchell, for help with the illustrations; Andy Owens; Richard Cassels, for information supplied; the staff of Chester County Record Office; the librarians of Birkenhead Central, Chester City, Congleton, Heswall, Wallasey Central, Winsford and Frodsham libraries, and last, but far from least, my wife Margaret, for her work as chauffeuse, ms-reader and general advisor.

NOBODY SAW ME!

The late 18th century was a time of social and economic uncertainty, particularly for working folk. Comparatively few were able to contemplate the future with the same sort of firm assurance as 29-year-old John Thornhill at the beginning of 1797.

Thornhill was butler and general servant to the rector of Lymm, the Reverend Peter Egerton Leigh, and his wife, Theodosia. A tall, strong young man, he was honest, diligent, efficient and conscientious in the performance of his duties. Over the seven years he had worked for them, his employers had come to value these good qualities, and to appreciate Thornhill's unfailingly smart appearance and pleasant manner. So much so that they had almost come to regard him as a sort of son. He was also popular with the other members of the Leighs' large domestic staff. Out and about in the village on the rector's business, dressed in his striking outdoor livery of a purple and black jacket, light grey coat, red cape and black tricorn hat, he was generally regarded as a man of some consequence.

All that being so, Thornhill could have expected to have a roof over his head, clothes on his back, four meals a day, and something to jingle in his pockets, for as long as he chose to work for the rector. With the good references that would undoubtedly have been his if he had decided to move on, he might one day have hoped to secure the post of butler with some great family. In terms of the times in which he lived and the social position he occupied, John Thornhill was comfortable.

Added to his other blessings, his love-life had prospered, and he was engaged to be married to Mrs Leigh's personal maid, pretty Rebecca Clark.

Unfortunately for Thornhill, for all his advantages, he was not too bright and he was possessed of a quick temper when he felt threatened. Weaknesses that were to bring all his dreams to an end on the gallows.

In the late spring of 1797, Thornhill became, as he expressed it at his trial, 'concerned with Sally Statham, but once and once only'. The surname Statham appears to have been a sort of unofficial local name – almost certainly a reference to the Statham area of Lymm where she lived – used for a woman whose full name is entered in the parish burial register as Sarah Malone. Described at the trial as 'large and lusty', Sally, who was old enough to be Thornhill's mother, shared a cottage with another woman, Phoebe Daniels, and her own two children, and she earned a living by taking in washing. There was no mention of a husband at the trial, and there is no trace of one in the parish registers.

In June the rector and his wife travelled to Lichfield on church business, accompanied by some members of their staff, including John Thornhill and Rebecca Clark. Soon after they all returned, in October, Rebecca heard a rumour circulating in the village that Sally Statham was pregnant, and that her own fiancé was the man involved. When she tackled Thornhill with the allegation, he hotly denied it. Further, as a method of proving his innocence, he suggested that he and Rebecca should call at Sally's cottage and ask her personally to tell the truth of the matter. Somewhat mollified, Rebecca agreed.

It seems, however, that Thornhill was not prepared to leave the issue to chance. At some time during the following Sunday, he managed to spend a private half-hour with Sally, almost certainly tutoring her in what to say when he called with his fiancée, and possibly bribing her to say it.

That same evening, after church, the engaged couple called on the washerwoman. Told of the reason for their visit, Sally expressed astonishment, and said that she knew no more of Thornhill than '... the furthest man in London'. Rebecca was duly relieved and apologetic.

Unfortunately for John Thornhill, although he had managed to restore his fiancée's faith – at least for the moment – he could not quash the village rumours. Rumours that were continually fuelled, it seems, by Sally Statham, who delighted in telling all and sundry that Thornhill was the father of her unborn child.

The butler grew increasingly desperate. He was sure that if the rector found out about the situation, he would dismiss him from his post, and if Rebecca came to believe that he was the man responsible for Sally's condition, he would lose his fiancée.

Lymm. The black and white building in the foreground, the Dingle Hotel, was originally the rectory where John Thornhill was employed as butler and general servant.

Thornhill told the rectory gardener, John Pass, of his problem and fears.

Pass reminded Thornhill that Sally Statham was notoriously promiscuous, and had probably shared her bed with other men at about the same time as she had entertained him. Not only that, it was almost certainly possible to discover which men had been visiting Sally at the critical time. That being so, he suggested, the butler could claim that it was impossible to tell who had fathered the child. Thornhill answered that he had already thought of that, but even the admission that he had been intimate with the washerwoman was likely to lead to his dismissal and the loss of his fiancée.

The gardener next told Thornhill that if he had been faced with the butler's problem, he would have sent Sally back to her home parish, with £10 or £15 and instructions not to return to Lymm. This seems to have been a totally unrealistic suggestion. Where could the butler hope to find that sort of money when his total annual wage was probably less than £10?

The old year passed, and 1798 arrived, with Thornhill growing ever more desperate. So desperate that he decided that, if it became necessary, he would solve the problem by killing Sally.

To that end, he found some pretext to meet her on the wooded banks of the village lower dam on the night of 4th January. He prepared for the encounter by arming himself with a hammer. The two met, as arranged. Hot words were spoken, the butler lost his temper, produced the hammer, and rained blows down on Sally's head. When she appeared to be dead, he threw her body into the dam. It was an act not only of extreme wickedness, but of mind-boggling folly. To kill a woman with whom his name was currently being linked was to invite suspicion.

The following day, Sally Statham's body was spotted at about noon and dragged out of the water. She was fully dressed, apart from her petticoat and cap, and her shoes, which were found a month later weighed down with stones. The body was examined at her cottage by surgeons Billingham and Howard, of Knutsford, who came to the conclusion that she had been killed by three blows to the head. Blows which had been so savage that they had almost exposed the skull. They also discovered that she was about eight months pregnant.

Within hours, fingers were pointing at Thornhill.

Sheet-faced and trembling, the butler asked to speak to the rector. He told him that Sally Statham's body had been dragged out of the dam, and that he was suspected of having murdered her. He broke down in tears, crying, 'Nobody saw me. How can they prove anything against me?' He pleaded with his master to hide him, but the rector obviously saw the request as being beyond reason.

The following morning, Thornhill asked for an interview with Mrs Leigh. She saw the butler in the tea room. As he entered, she took one look at his face and then sank down into a chair. 'Oh God, John, I can see you are guilty,' she said. Thornhill fell to his knees in front of her and looked up, beseechingly, into her face. He begged her to conceal him so that the constables would not find him if they came to search the house. He said he would go to High Legh and catch the coach for London, or go to Liverpool and board a ship, where no one would be able to arrest him. When Mrs Leigh tried to convince him that escape was impossible, he said again, 'Nobody saw me.' He repeated the phrase, time after time.

That evening the parish constables came to the rectory and arrested Thornhill. They took him to the Spread Eagle, where he spent the night under lock and key. Next morning, for one reason or other, they brought him back to the rectory. There, he somehow escaped them, but he was spotted that same afternoon walking quickly through a field near High Legh. The constables managed to re-apprehend him, and that time they made no mistake: they took him straight to Chester city gaol.

During the 15 weeks he spent in prison, the butler held doggedly to the idea that if nobody had seen him commit the murder, he could not be convicted.

The trial opened on Friday, 20th April, presided over by two judges, the Honourable James Adair and the Honourable Francis Burton. Most of the witnesses were the butler's fellow servants, who had seen his gory condition on the night of 4th January, and the desperate attempts that he had made to clean the blood off his clothes. They testified to having seen blood on his jacket and trousers, on his shirt, stockings and even on his hat. They also spoke of his demented demeanour. Then there was his swollen and blistered right hand, for which he invented a variety of continually changing causes. When Rebecca asked him about it, he said that he had gone into the yard to drive off some pigs, and had fallen on the cinders. Questioned by the rector, he had said that he had fallen down in the dark, when going to 'the necessary'. He later altered the story to having stumbled while carrying some heavy coal.

Yet, in spite of all this damning evidence, Thornhill was convinced that he would be acquitted, because 'Nobody saw me'. So much so that his attitude throughout the proceedings was jaunty and light-hearted. Called on to speak in his defence, he simply said, 'I am innocent, and know nothing at all of the matter.'

It was only when he heard the death sentence being pronounced and saw the judges' black caps, that he suddenly crumbled. Sweat broke out on his face, and, if he had not been supported by the two warders who stood on each side of him in the dock, he would have collapsed. Even so, he refused to confess, presumably hoping against hope for a reprieve. Not that there was much time available for that. The trial finished on Saturday, and on the following Monday he was taken out to the place of execution at Boughton, where a large crowd waited to see the proceedings.

Then, on the gallows and in the last minutes of his life, Thornhill confessed to the minister appointed to comfort the condemned prisoners.

And, at about half-past one, he followed Sally Statham into eternity.

THE BEAUTY IN THE BATH

Cynthia Bolshaw was a sexual adventurer. Like all adventurers, she knowingly took risks, and, like many adventurers, she took one risk too many; a risk that brought her a violent death.

An attractive and vivacious divorcee from a well-to-do background, Cynthia was 50 when she met that death, but looked much younger. She lived in the small town of Heswall, on the Wirral Peninsula, and commuted daily to Chester, where she worked as a beautician in a large store. At both places she was known as an indefatigable socialite.

At about 10.15 am on Sunday, 8th October 1983, as they had previously arranged with Cynthia, her sister and her brother-in-law, Angela and David Stewart, called at the bungalow where she lived alone. As soon as they arrived they could see that something was wrong: the curtains were still drawn, the outside light over the front door was still on and Cynthia's red Toyota Corolla car was missing from the drive. They rang the bell, but there was no answer. They then went round to the back of the bungalow. They found the back door unlocked, and let themselves into the kitchen. It was in a state of uncharacteristic disorder, with a pan of milk on the cold stove, dishes on the worktops, and the fridge standing open. Alarmed, they called out. Receiving no reply, they went into the bedroom, where they found the bedclothes piled on the bottom of the bed, and Cynthia's personal clothing neatly folded nearby. There were patches of blood on the walls.

They found Cynthia's body in the bath, face down in the water, naked, apart from a necklace and a pair of earrings. The police could find no evidence of a forced entry, and it was clear that Cynthia had entertained a visitor because there were two glasses on a table, together with open bottles of sherry and brandy. There was also evidence of sexual activity, in the form of semen stains on Cynthia's black nightdress. Enquiries were to suggest that the visitor may have been unexpected, because Cynthia had told a workmate, whom she had dropped off at the nearby town of Neston at 6.20 pm on the previous evening, that she intended to spend a quiet evening alone.

A damp patch on the bed, where Cynthia had emptied her bladder as she was being throttled to death, revealed that the murderer had strangled her in the bedroom – apparently with his bare hands – before carrying the body into the bathroom and laying it in the bath. Severe bruises to her face and body and the blood patches on the bedroom walls indicated that she had first been subjected to a terrible beating.

Appointed to lead the investigation, Detective Superintendent Jim Owens of Merseyside Police checked the contents of the bungalow with Cynthia's adult son, Christopher. They discovered that a quantity of jewellery was missing. They also came across fourteen diaries and three address books, containing the names and addresses of many men. In the subsequent newspaper reports, the number varied between two hundred and four hundred – but, by any account, it amounted to an impressive total. Not only that, including, as it did, a number of prominent local businessmen, a captain in the Sultan of Oman's army, a magician who Cynthia met on a train, an inspector in the Ugandan police, a man who worked on the oil rigs, and a customs officer, it was a list that was also rendered remarkable by the mind-boggling variety of the individuals noted.

When the case eventually reached court, a life-long friend, Valerie Johnson-Hamer, was to explain, 'Cynthia had steady

Cynthia Bolshaw was an attractive and vivacious divorcee.

relationships, but between them, she met other men and had sex with them on a very casual basis. She was a very highly-sexed woman ...'.

The media soon dubbed the crime 'The Beauty in the Bath Murder'.

An inquiry was launched, involving some hundred officers. First to be questioned were those men listed in Cynthia's diaries and address books – at least those who still lived in this country – and then the questioning moved on to house-to-house visits at Heswall, and at the village of Burton, seven miles away, where Cynthia had lived until some seven months previously. An inquiry which brought no quick leads.

In the meantime, Cynthia's missing car had been found six miles away in a field gateway off the A540 in the direction of Chester. In fact, it had been found before the murder was discovered by an off-duty police officer, who had noted its presence as he had been driving along the road early on the Sunday morning. When they examined the car closely, the police found that the petrol tank was full and the keys were in the ignition. One of Cynthia's neighbours, Mrs Iris Elliott, told the police that she had seen the car still parked in its usual place on Cynthia's drive when she went to bed at 11.30 pm that Saturday evening. A broadcast appeal for information brought a witness forward who had seen a smartly-dressed man running across the A540 in the area where the car was found, at about 12.50 am on the Sunday morning.

Enquiries at Chester, where Cynthia worked, brought information from an assistant in an estate agents' office to the effect that, a week or so before the murder, Cynthia had been asking about properties in the Handbridge area of the city. She had been in the company of a man who the informant described as being aged 45 to 55, well-dressed and clean-shaven.

Appeals in the media for the running man and the man at the estate agents' office to come forward brought no responses.

The discovery of the missing jewellery on the Tuesday following the murder, wrapped in paper in a telephone booth at Marple, near Manchester, led to extensive police enquiries, over several weeks, in the Manchester area. They brought no results, and the police came to the conclusion that they had been left in a place where they were certain to be found, and (with the luck that did in fact bless the ploy) handed in to the police, and the investigation diverted from the Wirral Peninsula.

After some four months, with all the likely British avenues tried, the local police enlisted the assistance of Interpol to secure the questioning of those British men on Cynthia's list who had moved to work overseas, and of the foreigners listed. It was a search that took the enquiries to Japan, Uganda, Dubai, Germany, France and the United States. This extension to the inquiry also drew a blank.

The search dragged into weeks, and then months, until it was, of necessity, scaled-down, but it was not abandoned. Far from it. For fifteen years, the murder incident room at Heswall police station maintained a repository where all the existing evidence was stored under lock and key. Included in that evidence was a total of something like 1,000 statements. For fifteen years the police left no possible leads untried. In doing so, they, inevitably perhaps, followed what turned out to be a number of false trails and blind alleys.

Equally important, as it eventually transpired, the local and regional media kept the case in the public eye by publicising any new direction taken by the police. In May 1997, for example, they reported that the case had been accepted by what was then a new database in Hampshire – 'Operation Enigma' – which is a catalogue of unsolved cases, with all the forensic details logged. The information is then cross-referenced to pick up patterns of serial killers. In the event, 'Enigma' was not able to provide a lead, but, speaking at the time, Detective Inspector Parry of Merseyside Police, who had been involved in the case from the beginning, said, 'The investigation is still very much alive, and because so many people knew Cynthia, I'm optimistic we'll get to the bottom of this, hopefully sooner rather than later.'

It was the publicity that the media gave to a new line of enquiry which led to the crucial breakthrough. In March 1999 they reported that, as a result of new advances in forensic science, it might be possible to assemble a DNA profile of Cynthia's killer from evidence collected from the murder scene. Those mentioned in Cynthia's diaries and address books were asked to come forward to donate saliva samples. Asked whether the police were prepared to exhume suspects who had died during the intervening years, for that purpose, Detective Superintendent David Smith refused to dismiss the possibility.

It did not come to that. Prompted by the media reports of this new development, Mrs Barbara Taft walked into Heswall Police Station to say she had some information about the Cynthia Bolshaw murder. In a statement, she said that, at the time of the crime, she had been married to John Edwin Taft, a double-glazing worker, from whom she had since been divorced. During the weekend that the murder was committed she had been away from home on a course at Sussex University. When she returned, the following weekend, her husband had told her that there had been a murder in Heswall. He said that the victim had been Cynthia Bolshaw, a woman Barbara Taft did not know. Taft said he was worried because he had been at Cynthia's house doing some work on the Saturday of the murder, and he was afraid that he would be accused of the crime. He told her that he had destroyed his sweater, jeans, and the shoes he had been wearing at Mrs Bolshaw's home, saying that he had burned the clothing and buried it in the garden. Barbara Taft said she had understood Taft had burned the clothing because those particular items might have been identified as belonging to someone who had been at the bungalow. He also told her

John Taft, sentenced to life imprisonment for the murder of Cynthia Bolshaw. (The Times)

that he had removed some pages from the works diary relating to work due to be done at Cynthia's home. She had refused her husband's plea to say, if she was interviewed by the police, that she had been at home the previous weekend. In the event, she had not been questioned.

The police had found Taft's business card during their search of the bungalow. Like hundreds of other men, he had been routinely questioned in the initial stages of the investigation, but, at that time, his claim that he did not know Cynthia had satisfied the officers who had interviewed him.

John Taft, aged 49, by then a director of a Birkenhead double-glazing company, was arrested by Murder Squad detectives and charged with the crime. Described in the newspapers as a neat, slim, grey-haired figure, he denied killing Cynthia Bolshaw, but responded to all questions with a blanket 'No comment'. He appeared before a magistrate's court on 11th April 1999, when he was remanded in custody, to await trial at Liverpool Crown Court. His application for bail was refused.

The trial opened on 10th November 1999. Presenting the case for the Crown, Andrew Edis QC claimed that Taft had strangled Cynthia, and had taken some jewellery to suggest that the motive for the crime had been robbery. He had then driven her car for six miles along the A540, parked it in the field gateway where it had been found, and then walked back to Heswall along the Wirral Way – a country park laid out on the bed of a dismantled railway. He had left the jewellery at Marple in an attempt to draw the police investigation away from Heswall. Significantly, the telephone box where the jewellery had been found was on Taft's route to his firm's head office in Manchester. Mr Edis also told the court that a DNA blood sample taken from Taft matched the semen stains found on Cynthia's nightdress.

Denying the charge, Taft admitted that he had been involved in an affair with Cynthia. He had visited her on the evening of 7th October 1983 at her home, and they had 'made love'. He claimed that when he left, at about 10.30 pm, Cynthia had been unharmed and cheerful. He first heard about the crime on the Monday morning, he said.

The trial lasted until 26th November, when, after some twelve hours of deliberations, the jury reached a 10–2 majority 'Guilty' verdict. Taft looked stunned at the decision, and then broke down in tears, holding his head in his hands.

Sentencing him to life imprisonment, Judge David Clark QC, the Recorder of Liverpool, said, 'You have been convicted by the jury of murdering Cynthia Bolshaw in 1983. Why you killed her will never be known, except by you. What is clear, however, is that you kept quiet all these years and have never told the truth about what happened that night. You are an intelligent and calculating man who, as far as I can see, has shown no remorse.'

As the judge announced the sentence, Christopher Bolshaw, the victim's only child, and his wife, Gaynor, hugged each other in the court's public gallery.

Taft was taken to prison, still protesting his innocence.

THE GHOSTS OF BACKFORD HALL

'**B**ackford Hall is probably the most haunted building on Wirral, and possibly in the whole of Cheshire,' says Mike McManus. It is an informed opinion. As Chairman of the Supernatural Encounters Association based in Ellesmere Port, and a former Chairman of Wirral Paranormal Investigations, over the past five years or so Mike has organised and attended many psychic research vigils at locations throughout the county, as well as at places further afield.

His interest in Backford Hall was aroused by a feature article published in the *Liverpool Daily Post*, which outlined some of the eerie incidents that various people have reported at the Hall within living memory. These have included the sound of horses' hooves over non-existent cobbles, the feel of clutching spectral hands, and a normally-placid dog that was too terrified to enter the Hall: incidents which seemed to have revealed the existence of restless spirits confined to a building that, according to local tradition, has witnessed at least one murder and three suicides. The article persuaded Mike that Wirral Paranormal Investigations should launch an investigation of Backford Hall as soon as possible.

The present Hall is the second to occupy the site. The first, built in 1571, was demolished in 1863 by the Lord of the Manor, Edward Holt Glegg, who replaced it with the present Jacobean-style building we see today. In 1946

Backford Hall was acquired by Cheshire County Council, and adapted for its current use as offices.

Only rarely are those working at the Hall subjected to anything that might be regarded as a supernatural experience. The most notable of such incidents occurred in 1994 when a cleaner, Mrs Pauline Drake, was busy in the old stable block. 'Something touched me on the shoulder,' she reported. 'It felt cold, like someone had put their hand on my shoulder. I turned around and there was no one there. With all the history in this place, I would say it was a ghost.'

WPI obtained permission from Steve Brown, the Administrative Manager of the Hall, to hold an overnight vigil with the object of discovering whether they could detect any more definite signs of psychic activity there at night.

Most psychic research groups conduct their vigils in accordance with a well-established, widely-used system. Like similar groups elsewhere, to ensure that its research is as accurate as possible, and to acquire as much hard evidence as possible, WPI possesses a wide range of equipment, ranging from state-of-the-art camcorders to the basic, but invaluable, notebooks. Other items include cameras, a sound monitor system – basically the same as a baby-listening arrangement – which allows sound made in one area to be heard by an observer listening in another, thermometers, tape and digital recorders and torches.

Having decided on the property to be investigated, one or two members of the group interview anyone who has had any experience that may have been psychic in origin at the property, to establish, as it were, the known situation before the WPI team mounts its observation vigils. In the case of Backford Hall, the main subjects were Mrs Drake and a caretaker, Sid Hawes. Although Mr Hawes, who has worked at the Hall for many years, is a complete disbeliever, he has yet to find a good, logical, reason to explain why an alsatian he once owned would flatly refuse to go into the building through the main entrance, and would stand, feet firmly planted on the threshold, with its ears back and hackles raised. Less specifically, a few members of staff admitted to a strange feeling of uneasiness that they experience in some parts of the building, particularly the reception area and the back stairs – formerly the servants' stairs.

As soon as the selected team arrive at the location to be investigated, they look round the place to familiarise themselves with its layout, and to choose the best places to set up the equipment. This decision can depend on the existence of 'cold spots' – a phenomenon often reported in haunted buildings and consisting of areas of up to two or even three square metres where a distinct fall in temperature may be measured. Next, the team choose a room to use as a base, where they can take breaks from observation and fortify themselves with hot drinks. Last among these preliminary preparations is the choice of areas where members are to sit and observe, and the allocation of those areas to individuals. The seating is always arranged in a way that allows every member to see another member, for purposes of mutual support.

The WPI's chosen team of eight held their first vigil at Backford Hall on 7th June 1997. They arrived at the Hall at about 8.30 pm. As soon as they entered the door, they all felt a strange heaviness in their chests, which persisted for an hour or so, before it wore off.

First, they established their base in a conference room on the ground floor. They then chose what they judged to be the best spots for the individual investigators to sit during the vigil, and the best places to set up the electronic equipment. As they moved about, in the course of this work, some members reported encountering 'cold spots'. The team settled down at 11.15 pm, each observer in his/her designated place. Five members were stationed in the cellar – a huge basement area incorporating four large rooms. Two

Backford Hall. (Photo, Mike McManus)

others were stationed near to the Hall reception area, and the other on the landing.

At 11.59 pm the team heard the sound of two loud thuds – apparently from the ground floor area. The house fell silent for a few seconds, and then the noise came again. A phenomenon that occurred at irregular intervals throughout the night, it was captured on four tape recorders.

At 1.17 am Barry Lowe, stationed near the gallery/landing, noticed a strong smell of lavender, which persisted for a few minutes. Summoned to offer their opinions, three other members were also able to catch the scent.

Suddenly, at 2.18 am, the main, very heavy door at the top of the cellar stairs, which had been standing open, slammed shut, startling Pam Hendrikson, who was sitting close to it. She called to the other four members in the cellar, Adam Khan, Mark O'Driscoll, Niki Smith and John Stevens. They hurried across to her. John opened the door again and all five members in the cellar then watched to see if it would slam shut a second time. Six minutes later, whatever force was working on it obliged and, witnessed by all five observers, the door crashed shut again. Again, John opened it, and that time he wedged it open with a small piece of wood. In spite of the wedge, at 3 am the door slammed shut for a third time. Again, the slamming door was both seen and heard by all five observers in the area. The sound was caught on tape. John called upstairs to the other three observers, and asked Mike to bring the camcorder down to the cellar. In the way of these things, after Mike arrived, ready to catch the slamming door on tape, the door remained inert and open, with the teasing spirit totally uncooperative for the remainder of the vigil. Other sounds noted and recorded during the night included those of a woman laughing, children giggling and distinct, heavy, sighs.

That first vigil ended at 7 am, with the team determined to hold another, in an attempt to identify the spirits they had encountered.

It was not, however, until more than a year later, on 25th July 1998, that they returned to mount a second vigil. With the building owned by Cheshire County Council, and with any arrangement for an all-night watch involving serious matters of insurance and security, the WPI committee decided to be diplomatic about the approaches it made to the site manager for permission to hold another nocturnal session.

During this second vigil, the observers heard the same sort of occasional banging sounds as they had heard during their first. Again, they caught the sound of children giggling. Two observers, Mark O'Driscoll and Barry Lowe, heard the sound of a dog howling and the padding of its paws on floorboards, somewhere close to them.

The most exciting observation made during this vigil was, however, the sight of ghostly figures on the stairs. At 11.00 pm Carolyn Bristow, stationed near to the top of the main stairs, heard two dull thuds. Immediately afterwards, she became aware of two figures coming up the stairs. One was a woman dressed in an 18th-century-style pink dress, with a cream, laced and striped bodice, and wearing a grey wig; the other was a man. They appeared to be real – not the sort of semi-transparent figures favoured by ghost film-makers. After a few seconds, they faded away. The woman in the pink dress was seen again by another observer, Denise Jones, at 2.14 am. Denise was stationed in the gallery/landing area at the top of the stairs when the spectral lady passed her – alone on that occasion – and proceeded to descend the stairs. She faded away about halfway down, after she had been visible for about 30 seconds.

An account of this vigil, which was published in the *Ellesmere Port Standard*, brought Mike two interesting and very helpful letters from Mrs Carol Holmes, who had lived at the Hall as a small child between 1951 and 1954, when her father, Jim Walker, had been the caretaker. Mrs Holmes wrote that during the time her family lived at the Hall the lady with the grey wig was seen on several occasions, both in the corridors and in the grounds by the pool. Mrs Holmes stated that she, personally, saw the figure standing by the pool, amid an expanse of bluebells, and that, even more than 40 years later, she only had to see a bluebell carpet to be reminded of that particular scene. She also had a suggestion to make about the possible identity of the phantom dog heard in the Hall. Could it be, she wondered, the ghost of a collie that her father had owned? Shep was very much a one-man dog. Although he was devoted to his master, he looked at the rest of the world through his red eyes, and hated it. As a child, Mrs Holmes had been terrified of the creature. When the time came for the family to leave the Hall, Jim, reluctantly, had the dog destroyed because he was convinced that, with its malevolent temperament, it could not be rehoused.

In the early autumn of 1998, for a variety of reasons, a number of members decided to leave WPI and to form a new group, to be known as the 'Supernatural Encounters Association'. Mike McManus was elected Chairman. It was this new group which continued the work at Backford Hall.

A third vigil was held on 14th/15th November 1998. Again, banging and sighs were heard and recorded. The lavender smell was again noted. At 5 am five members of the team held a seance in the gallery area. Two loud raps were heard in response to the question 'Do you have a name?', but attempts to discover the name failed. During this seance all five team members saw a grey, misty, small cloud-like shape appear in a corridor off the gallery. It lingered there for about a minute, before fading away.

A fourth vigil was held on 10th/11th April 1999. The team heard, and recorded, the by-then familiar banging and sighs, which occurred occasionally throughout the night. At 11.28 pm the equally-familiar lavender smell was also noted by four members around the gallery/landing and in the top corridor. It persisted for about a minute.

At 9.20 pm Mike McManus was engaged in setting up the camcorder in the gallery, while the other team members were all downstairs in the conference room – which they were using as a base – when he heard a female voice, close at hand, say 'Dave'. He went downstairs and told the others what had happened. Dave Williams left the room, but returned a few minutes later to ask who had called him. He said he had heard his name called twice. No one else had left the room during his absence.

Stationed in the long corridor, at about 11.20 pm Mike saw a vague, grey, misty shape, moving away from him and in the direction of the old servants' stairs. Barry Lowe and Mark O'Driscoll were posted at points where they could also see this phenomenon, which was visible for some two minutes.

At about 12.30 am Mike was sitting at the bottom of the back stairs when he heard what sounded like a woman's

The strange column of white mist which appeared in the reception area of Backford Hall at about 2 am on 11th April 1999. It was seen by six observers who were seated on the gallery/landing immediately above it. As they watched, it moved out through a wall and returned. Then it moved through a closed door and came back, before it faded away. It was visible for two or three minutes. The disc-shaped object is the top of a light shade. (Photo, Dave Williams)

dress rustling along the landing, followed by the sound of a woman laughing. He went up the stairs and, as he did so, he could still hear the rustling and the laughter. At the top of the stairs, he encountered Dave Williams and Mark O'Driscoll, who had also heard the laughter. At 2 am six members of the team began a seance round a table placed on the gallery, immediately overlooking the reception area. Suddenly, they became aware of a column of white mist moving in the reception area. As they watched, it passed through a wall and returned. Then it passed through a closed door and came back. It was seen by all six members present, and Dave Williams took a photograph of it.

Another seance brought an equally impressive demonstration of a supernatural presence. At 5.45 am three members, John Millington, Carolyn Bristow and Simon Cooney, sat round a large, very heavy, table in one of the ground floor offices. During the seance, the table began to vibrate, and then one end lifted clear off the floor, down again and up again, and continued to do so. The phenomenon was so unnerving that John and Carolyn left the room. After a minute or two John returned, accompanied by Mike McManus, who had heard the table banging. The table continued to lift – a clear inch from the floor – and fall again, and Mike checked that no one was moving it with their legs. The phenomenon continued for five to ten minutes. During this time, strange shadows were seen flickering about the office door.

The vigil ended at 6.30 am, but one more piece of evidence awaited the team. Later, when they played back a tape from a recorder, which had been positioned in the ground floor corridor, close to the reception area, they heard a female voice speaking the names 'Ann', 'Joseph' and 'Lucy'.

Having so far amassed a wealth of material the SEA is now faced with the challenge of trying to identify the Hall's ghosts. Who were these spirits in their mortal lives?

An obvious line of inquiry was to discover the name of the murder victim, and those of the three suicides, and, perhaps, see if any of them matched the names on the tape. Unfortunately, there appears to be no information, in the form of dates or names, that would allow the incidents to be located in the parish register and other records. The tedious business of trawling through these documents at the Cheshire Record Office has begun, but, so far, without results. A number of tombstones which bear the three names heard on the tape have been noted in Backford parish churchyard, but there is nothing to indicate whether any particular one was associated with the Hall. And they are, after all, reasonably common names. Were the murder/suicide stories no more than that – stories?

So, the mystery remains and the search continues. Burglaries at the Hall in 1999 and 2000, involving the theft of several thousand pounds' worth of computer equipment, rendered the problem of obtaining permission to hold further vigils more difficult. But it is a very intriguing situation – perhaps even one more all-night watch will produce some clear answers!

CHERCHEZ LA FEMME

Peter Steer was hanged at Boughton, Chester, on Monday, 24th April 1786. He was hanged for poisoning his wife, in an attempt to clear his way to marrying his teenage lover. It must be one of the most clumsy premeditated murders in the criminal history of the county. From reports of the evidence given at the trial, which appeared in the *Chester Chronicle* of 28th April 1786, it is possible to trace the course of the murder almost from the time it was conceived in Steer's mind until his arrest; his prison cell confession is only needed to cross the 't's and dot the 'i's. From that evidence, it is clear that, even in the preliminary stages of the crime, he left clues that might well have aroused suspicions. That they did not do so until days after the murder was committed may have had something to do with the fact that he lived in a predominantly God-fearing Quaker community that was open in its ways, and reluctant to gossip and harbour suspicions of anyone; a community which, collectively, always tried to think the best of people.

Peter Steer, who was 39 at the time of the murder, and his wife, Phoebe, who was three years older, had been married for 17 years. They lived in the hamlet of Morley, near Mobberley, with their four children, Alice who was almost 14 at the time of the murder, Sarah who was 9, Thomas who was 6 and Elizabeth who was 3. As a casual day labourer, Steer's earnings would have been modest, but he had married well, in as much as Phoebe was a daughter of a prosperous family of corn merchants, and they were, therefore, able to live in some comfort.

Steer's journey to the gallows began in the spring of 1784, when he met 14-year-old Sarah Barrow, who had recently started work as a servant to his widowed brother-in-law, corn merchant Thomas Cash, and his unmarried sister, Mary, at their farmstead. Steer often worked for Cash, and, in the months that followed, he frequently found himself working side by side with the pretty girl. He became besotted with her, and when the opportunity arose he seduced her. In court she said it had been about a year after she started work at the farm that he first made advances to her. She was turning the cornflour in the barn in which he was winnowing when he took her in his arms, showered her with kisses and said that he wished she was his wife. Their first sexual encounter occurred about a week later, when she and Steer were milking in the cowshed. She said Steer took hold of her laid her down on the floor and forced her to have intercourse. At his trial she was to claim that Steer had raped her, but, significantly, the severity of the rape can be judged from the fact that she said she did not call out too loudly for fear that her master would hear, and, equally significantly, from the fact that when the act was finished they both carried on with the milking.

Over the next year or so, they met as frequently as they could, in circumstances which they must have imagined to be of secrecy, to have intercourse. According to Sarah's evidence, they often met on Sunday mornings, either at the Steers' or the Cashs' house, when Phoebe and her children and the Cashs were at the Quaker Meeting House.

During the 18th century most of the families living in the hamlet of Morley, and many of those living in the surrounding area of Mobberley and Wilmslow, including Thomas and Mary Cash, were Quakers – that is, members of the Society of Friends. The Steers and Sarah's parents, the Barrows, however, were among those regular attenders who had yet to be admitted into full membership of the Society. It would have been strange if some had not noticed Peter and Sarah's frequent absences, and added two and two together. Indeed, John Ardern, a local tailor, testified in court that, even before Phoebe's death, he had heard that there was 'some connection' between the two. The talk, such as it was, may well have been muted by a Quaker predilection to believe that there could have been an innocent reason for the absences. Whatever the talk, Phoebe seems to have been oblivious of it.

In passing, it should be noted that, reprehensible as it was for Steer to commit adultery and to form a sexual liaison with a girl 25 years his junior and who was only 18 months older that his own oldest child, he was not committing a criminal offence because, at the time, the age of consent was 12.

By November 1785 Steer had decided to remove the main obstacle to his marrying Sarah by murdering his wife. The method he chose was arsenic poisoning.

Steer launched his plan on Friday, 18th November. He arrived home complaining that he felt unwell, and said that if he was not feeling better by the following day, he would go to see a doctor at Knutsford. Came the Saturday, and Steer announced that he was going to Knutsford.

At the trial, John Ardern, who had been doing some work at the Steers' home, testified that Phoebe had tried to persuade her husband to see Dr Jeffs, at Wilmslow, saying 'He can bleed you just as well.' Steer had rejected this suggestion, with the words, 'Jeffs knows nothing of the matter,' and he appeared to be set on going to Knutsford. At the time, Ardern had thought that it was an excuse to go to Knutsford to meet Sarah Barrow.

In fact, Steer made the journey to obtain the arsenic with which to poison his wife. He spent most of the day at Knutsford, not only buying the arsenic, but inadvertently providing a number of witnesses with enough fragments of evidence to help to cement the case against him at the trial.

On his way to Knutsford, Steer called at the Mobberley home of a shopkeeper friend, John Howarth, to deliver a note with the details of a 'harmless white powder' for a sick relation who was staying with the Howarths. It seems likely that Steer and Howarth had previously discussed the patient's sickness, and Steer had suggested some mild potion, the name of which he had later written on paper to give to Howarth. Steer then offered to accompany Howarth to Knutsford. The suggestion appears to have been an ill-conceived ruse to establish some sort of alibi, hoping that Howarth might vouch for him if questioned. Unfortunately for Steer, his use of the word 'harmless' struck Howarth as curious and, lodging in his memory, it was later to acquire an additional, sinister, significance, when it emerged that Phoebe had been murdered with a far from harmless white powder.

At Knutsford, they called at an apothecary's, where Howarth bought the 'harmless white powder'. They then went on to the Royal George, where they had two or three pints of beer. In fact, they seem to have spent most of the day in a pub crawl but, at various times, Steer slipped out for short periods, on one pretext or another. On one of those occasions he said he had been to see Dr Howard, who had let some blood to relieve his cold (blood-letting being a standard treatment for a variety of ailments at the time).

On that or another of his excursions, he bought the arsenic. At the trial, the prosecution was to suggest that, thinking that, having already had some dealings with Dr Howard, there was a good chance that Howard might have a clear recollection of his buying the poison, Steer went, instead, to a surgeon, William Billingham. In doing so, he made a bad mistake.

While it is impossible to assess what sort of witness Howard would have made, it is difficult to imagine that anyone could have made a better one than Billingham. Very obviously, the surgeon was nobody's fool and, equally obviously, he was a man with a social conscience. Questioned at the trial, he was able to testify that, between

Knutsford (circa 1900). The pub on the right is the Royal George, *where Peter Steer spent some time on 19th November 1785 considering how to obtain the arsenic with which to kill his wife.* (Collection of Paul Mitchell).

3 and 4 pm on Saturday, 19th November, a man he did not know, aged about 40, came into his shop and asked for two pennyworth of white arsenic. Billingham asked the customer's reason for wanting the poison. 'To kill rats,' was the reply. He then asked the man's name. 'Heald of Mobberley,' was the reply. As a surgeon, Billingham knew a number of families named 'Heald' in the area, but he did not recognise the customer as being a member of any of them. Assailed by doubts, he made a careful mental note of the man's appearance, a precaution which enabled him to identify Steer, without any hesitation, as the customer who had bought the arsenic.

The decision to buy the arsenic from a supplier he did not know is another aspect of Steer's crime which demonstrated its essential clumsiness. Presumably, a more able schemer would have taken his time to study all the possible sources of the poison, in an attempt to locate an apothecary or doctor who was notoriously absent-minded or casual – preferably one whose business was as far away from Morley as possible – but, even if he had thought of it, Steer was not prepared to take his time: he wanted Sarah, and he wanted her quickly.

On what seems to have been the last of his forays, Steer bumped into the recently-widowed Josiah Barrow, a farmer, the father of Sarah, and a man he knew well. He invited the farmer to join him and Howarth for a drink at the Red Lion. Like Phoebe, Barrow appears to have been unaware of the relationship between Steer and his daughter.

At one point during their conversation in the pub, Barrow was more than a little surprised when Steer suddenly clapped him on the knee and said, 'Josiah thou art a widower, and I think I shall be one soon'. Barrow asked whether Phoebe was ill, but said, at the trial, that he could not recall Steer's answer. He later learned that there had been nothing wrong with Phoebe's health at the time. Barrow testified that when Steer left the other two men, to set off on the six-mile walk home, he seemed to be in good spirits.

The next morning – Sunday – Peter Steer, Phoebe and their four children sat down to a breakfast of frumenty – a sort of porridge-cum-cereal made with wholegrain wheat, milk, flour, currants and spices. Each was eating from their own bowl. As soon as she tried her frumenty, Phoebe said that it did not taste quite right, as if the wheat she had used to make it had been bad, but no one else noticed anything untoward. The taste was not, however, unpalatable enough to deter Phoebe from continuing to eat her portion.

One odd incident occurred during the meal, appearing trivial at the time, but recognised as sinister in retrospect. When Phoebe gave some of her frumenty to the youngest child, Elizabeth, Steer snatched it back and poured it into his wife's bowl again, with some disapproving comment.

After the fatal breakfast, Alice and the other children went to the Quaker meeting, at Morley. Perhaps Phoebe was already beginning to feel ill, because she decided not to go with them, but Alice testified that, when they left home, between 10 and 11 am, she appeared to be all right. When they returned three hours, or so, later, Phoebe told Alice that she felt ill and had been sick.

Alice sent her 9-year-old sister to tell Phoebe's brother, Thomas Cash, and her sister Mary of her illness. As soon as she heard the news, Mary came to see her sister. She found Phoebe upstairs in bed. It was obvious that she was very ill: she was a ghastly colour; she complained about severe abdominal pains; she was afflicted with a raging thirst; and, from time to time, she vomited large quantities of what Mary was to describe as '... a greenish water'. Mary made some tea for her, and did what she could to comfort her. She left as it was growing dark, leaving her sister to Steer's – unknown to her – evil ministrations. On Monday, Phoebe's condition grew steadily worse, with the pains growing ever more acute.

When Mary visited Phoebe again on the Tuesday afternoon, Alice told her that her mother had passed many loose, greenish stools. In evidence Mary was to testify that, when she arrived, Steer was shelling peas and appeared indifferent to his wife's suffering. Before she went home that evening, Mary suggested to Phoebe and Steer that, if there was no sign of improvement by morning, they should get a doctor to examine Phoebe. To that, Steer made a short, non-committal reply.

Later that same evening, a neighbour, Betty Pearson, called at the Steers', to see if she could help. During her stay Phoebe grew visibly worse, until Steer commented, 'I think she's going.' Betty rushed to the Cashs' farm to tell Phoebe's brother and sister that she appeared to be on the point of death. They hurried to the Steers', but, by the time they arrived, Phoebe was dead. Peter Steer was apparently grief-stricken, but Mary was later to claim that she detected something false in his lamentations.

Betty Pearson's daughter-in-law, Tabitha, was summoned to lay out the body. She arrived at about 1 am on Wednesday, and, accustomed as she was to dealing with cadavers, she was astonished to find the corpse grossly bloated.

Just after 4 am, Betty and Tabitha Pearson roused the local carpenter and coffin maker, Samuel Goodyear, to measure the corpse. In the event, Goodyear must have had a number of coffins in stock and a good idea of Phoebe's build, because he brought a coffin with him. By the time the Pearsons returned with Goodyear, the house seems to have been crowded with neighbours and relations.

Like Tabitha, Goodyear was struck by the swollen condition of the body. Not only that, as he started to lift Phoebe into the coffin, her head fell back and a large quantity of greenish matter poured out of her mouth, nostrils and ears – a phenomenon that neither he nor Tabitha, nor anyone else present had seen before. After another neighbour, Hannah Strettell, had wiped the mess from Phoebe's head and face with a cloth, she turned to Steer, and asked him what his wife had eaten last. She had to repeat the question several times before he answered, 'A little small beer with sugar in it.'

Steer then caused something of a stir in the gathering by announcing his intention to arrange the funeral for the following day – Thursday. When Sam Goodyear asked why he was in such a hurry, he replied, 'I am afraid she might swell and be troublesome.' Meaning that the body might pass on whatever disease had caused Phoebe's death.

With some difficulty, he was persuaded to set the funeral for the Friday, 25th November 1785, to allow time for relations living some distance away to be notified of Phoebe's death, and to travel to Morley.

In spite of the Quaker reluctance to gossip or to think ill of others, it does seem strange that, even then, when the accumulated circumstantial evidence was so obvious, no one appears to have voiced any suspicions. There was the talk about Steer's relationship with Sarah; his comment to Barrow that he soon expected to be a widower, made when Phoebe was in good health; his apparent indifference to his wife's suffering noticed by a number of those who had visited or attended her during her last few days; his lack of concern at the loss of his wife – in his evidence given at the trial, five months later, Goodyear was to say that he 'marvelled at it', and the strange condition of the swollen body, issuing its 'green matter'.

If there were any suspicions, they were not developed and voiced as public accusations at that stage and, on the Friday, Phoebe was buried in the Quaker graveyard at Mobberley.

Obviously, Steer did not realise how many blunders he had made, or how fortunate he had been to escape detection up to that point. Apparently feeling secure in the knowledge that Phoebe was safe in the ground, he made one mistake too many.

It happened on Sunday, 4th December. That morning Steer encountered Sarah at the Quaker meeting. It was the first time they had met for a month or so, because Sarah had left Cash's employment at the beginning of November, and moved back to Mere, four miles away, to nurse a dying sister.

Giving evidence at Steer's trial, Sarah was to state that, later that day, she just happened to be riding past the Steers' house, with no intention of calling, when Fanny Jackson, a woman who seems to have been acting as a housekeeper and child-minder for Steer, came out and invited her in.

During Alice's evidence, she said that her father was upstairs when Sarah arrived, and she went up to him. They stayed upstairs for about half an hour. Sarah stayed for tea, sitting at the table with Steer, his children and Fanny Jackson. It was then that Steer made his final, reckless, fatal, mistake. Alice told the court that Fanny had used japanned tea-tongs to hand out the food. Turning to Sarah, Steer said, 'When we are married we will have silver tea-tongs.' For

Fanny and Alice, at least, the comment must have been crystal clear in its implications.

While Steer's pronouncement would not have had the same significance for Sarah as it had for the others – she had been at Mere during the whole period of the events surrounding the murder – she did not welcome it. She made that clear to Steer after tea, when he drew her into the parlour and asked her to marry him. She refused point-blank. Possibly, she had been happy enough to have a sexual fling with an older man who was safely married, but the idea of marrying a widower 25 years older than she was did not appeal. For Steer, besotted with Sarah Barrow and conscious that he had committed murder to gain her, the refusal must have been devastating.

He tried again. When Sarah left, Steer walked with her for a half mile or so, and again asked her to marry him. That time she told him, in an off-hand way, that she would think about it, before riding off.

The report of Steer's 'silver tongs' comment spread rapidly among the local community of Morley and the surrounding area. Like a match, it lit up the other clues that had littered his murderous progress, and revealed them, collectively, as potent evidence of his guilt.

Such was the pressure of public conjecture and speculation that, on Saturday, 10th December, Phoebe's body was exhumed for the purposes of a post-mortem examination. Dr Howard was appointed to perform the examination, with the assistance of Surgeon Billingham.

The two medical men presented their findings at the inquest held on Thursday, 15th December 1785. They stated that they had found a quantity of white powder in the body's stomach, small intestine and abdomen. Although it was not a sufficient quantity for them to apply what they termed 'the usual test', they believed the powder to be arsenic, a conviction that was reinforced by the condition of the body. They stated that, if the powder was indeed arsenic, there was forty times more than the lethal dose in the body. That being so, they offered their professional opinion that Mrs Phoebe Steer had been poisoned.

The other witnesses questioned included Alice Steer, Mary Cash, Betty and Tabitha Pearson, and Peter Steer himself. Not surprisingly, Steer denied all knowledge of the poison. At the end of the hearing, the coroner, John Hollins, recorded a verdict of wilful murder.

Steer was arrested, and imprisoned at Chester City goal, to await trial at the Spring Session of the Assizes.

When the trial opened, on Friday, 21st April 1786, Steer pleaded guilty. The key witnesses included his daughter Alice, Sarah Barrow, Josiah Barrow, Mary Cash, John Howarth, Betty Pearson, John Ardern, Sam Goodyear and the two medical men, Dr Howard and Mr Billingham. Their evidence left the jury no room for doubt, and the judge duly passed the death sentence.

A report of the execution appeared in the *Chester Chronicle* of 28th April: '... at the time appointed, this unfortunate man was taken to the place of execution amidst a prodigious concourse of spectators, where, after due time spent in prayer, the judgment of the law was put into execution, and his remains were delivered to an eminent surgeon for dissection. His behaviour after condemnation was marked with every appearance of penitence and resignation; and in his last moments he evinced a becoming sensibility of his unhappy situation.'

From the earliest times and until the middle of the 19th century, most executions in this country were public spectacles and, by the 18th century, they had generated a complementary thriving street trade in broadsides (leaflets) purporting to offer details of the story behind the crime and execution, some which may have originated with the criminal concerned and others which were written by the publishers to suit the prevailing popular taste. More often than not, it would seem, they were a mixture of both.

Part of the broadside which was sold on Chester streets within hours of Peter Steer's execution on 24th April 1786. (Courtesy of Manchester Central Library)

One such broadside, which appeared on the streets of Chester within hours of Steer's death, offers something of a postscript to the crime. It contained what the publisher claimed were the condemned man's dying speech and confession, and a copy of what was claimed to be the letter Steer wrote to his brother from prison. While the veracity of much that was published in broadsides was questionable, some of the passages that appeared do seem to have the ring of authenticity. It was in the letter to his brother, dated 21st April 1786, that Steer was said to have confessed: '... first, I gave her [Phoebe] a small quantity of arsenic in some frumenty. Secondly, I gave her some more arsenic the same night in buttermilk and water.' He also owned up to his affair with Sarah Barrow, and it seems that, pathetically, he had formed the idea that she would have run away with him. 'Sarah Barrow, she is the girl I was concerned with, and knows all these things, and would have gone with me out of the country. We went on very wickedly for twelve months together. She very frequently came to my bed when she could pick an opportunity to lie with me.'

The broadside also alleged that Steer tried to cheat the executioner by attempting to hang himself in his cell; clearly, if it was true, it was yet another – almost certainly, the last – project he managed to bungle.

THE MYSTERY OF THE
WALLASEY HERMIT

Even before the news appeared in the local newspaper, word that the Hermit was dead had spread throughout Wallasey.

Although little was known about him, for some 30 years Frederick Kreuger had been a familiar figure about the town: a stooped individual, with a drooping moustache, dressed in shabby clothes and, throughout all those years, of indeterminate age. Very occasionally he was glimpsed in the streets, but more often he was seen on the local beach, walking his dogs along the sands, and throwing sticks for them to chase. He always had a number of retrievers: sometimes as few as three, sometimes as many as six.

He arrived in Wallasey about 1877. For ten years or so he lived in what was described at the inquest on his death as 'various types of make-shift dwellings on various sites', before moving into a corrugated hut on the site of the new Wallasey Golf Club links, off Green Lane. There, he lived alone, apart from his dogs, for the last 20 years of his life. When the golf club was founded in 1891, Kreuger was already established on the course, and his tiny patch of a garden became out of bounds for the eighth hole – a situation that lasted, incidentally, until 1953, when the rule was abandoned.

Kreuger kept very much to himself, avoiding human contact as far as possible, a preference which, together with his distinctive appearance and marked foreign accent, led to widespread gossip and speculation. Possibly in a sort of impromptu collective attempt to categorise him, at a time when English society was obsessed with social pigeon-holes, he became known as 'the Hermit', and his home, inevitably, became known as the 'Hermit's Hut'.

The general curiosity about Kreuger persisted to the extent that the local newspaper sent a journalist to interview him in 1905. The paper's readers learned that the internal dimensions of the Hermit's Hut were 15 ft long, 9 ft wide and 12 ft high. It was divided into three compartments, which were sparsely furnished, but with every available space occupied by books and papers. These included volumes on classical subjects in Latin and Greek, and many musical scores by composers like Mozart and Wagner, and some which had been composed by Kreuger himself. The journalist also reported that Kreuger had told him that he lived on a small allowance that he received from Germany, and he quoted him as saying, 'I have no friends. I wish to exist alone. All I desire is the right to pass my days in study and contemplation.'

Those who judged by appearances guessed that the allowance must have been very small indeed.

'Mr Kreuger', commented the reporter, 'lives metaphorically speaking in the clouds'. The revelations probably stimulated more curiosity than they satisfied. Why would a man who could read classical writers in the original and who could compose music cut himself off from society, and live in poverty?

Of course, Kreuger could not avoid human contact completely. He still had to buy the basic necessities of life – food for himself and his dogs, oil for his lamp, and so on – and he could hardly have avoided exchanging the time of day with those who made a point of speaking to him in the street. It seems that many of those who did come into contact with him were much taken by his old world courtesy, which may have been why some locals went out of their way to offer him gifts of food and cast-off clothes. Gifts that he always accepted with great dignity. So much so that when the coroner at the inquest on Kreuger's death asked witness PC James Snelson whether these items could be described as 'the fruits of begging', the officer replied with as much warmth as he dared, 'You cannot call it begging; people used to give them to him out of charity.'

It seems that Kreuger was widely accepted by Wallasey residents as a character, and, as such, generally regarded with a degree of collective affection. Even so, the only person with whom he had any frequent dealings was Samuel Howard, a market gardener who lived in Green Lane. Such as it was, Kreuger's mail – mostly from Germany – was received addressed 'care of Howard', and Kreuger also called at the market gardener's house two or three times every week to collect fresh water.

During early March 1909, Charles Webster, a labourer at the market garden, was working in a field next to the Hermit's Hut. As he worked, he occasionally glimpsed Kreuger pottering about the hut, or coming and going, usually with his dogs.

On 8th March, however, Webster realised that he had not seen the Hermit for a couple of days. He went to the hut, and found two of Kreuger's dogs wandering about in the tiny garden. He knocked on the door and called, but there was no answer. He tried again. Still there was no reply. He then peered through the window, and saw Kreuger's legs sticking into view on the floor. He tried the door, but found it was locked.

He reported the matter to the local police station, and then returned to the hut with PC Robert Gilpin. The officer broke down the door, and they found Kreuger dead, kneeling on the floor, with his head resting on the sofa. He was fully dressed, apart from his boots and outdoor coat. The hut, which was in a state of extreme squalor, contained little, apart from the Hermit's books and papers.

Despite the objections of his retrievers, Kreuger's body was removed and taken to the Poulton Reading Room in Limekiln Lane.

At the inquest on Kreuger's death, Dr T.W.A. Napier stated that he had carried out a post-mortem on the body and found that the deceased had suffered from a strangulated hernia and from peritonitis, which had been the cause of death. He had been dead for three or four days. The body had been in a very dirty state, and the left cheek had been bitten by rats.

All of which was fairly routine. Far from routine were the facts about Kreuger's background, which emerged from the documents found in the hut, from fragments contributed by various witnesses, and from information supplied by the German Consulate in Liverpool — facts which were stated in full for the first time at the inquest. They helped to construct a picture that was even more improbable than the

The funeral of Frederick Kreuger held on 13th March 1909. (Collection of Ian Boumphrey)

most bizarre of the speculations that had gathered about Kreuger over the years.

Gotthold Johann Friedrick Kreuger had been born at Meckleburg, in Prussia, about 1848. His father had been a member of the Prussian civil service, working on the personal staff of the King. After graduating from Berlin University, Frederick practised law for a time, combining that occupation with a parallel career as a concert pianist. At the inquest, Samuel Howard testified that he had heard the Hermit play the piano 'very finely' on a number of occasions – presumably when he had called for water, because he did not have a piano at the hut. Kreuger, it was revealed, had a gift for languages. Not only was he proficient in the classical tongues, he was also fluent in English, French and Italian. It was probably this aptitude for languages that led him to enter the German diplomatic corps shortly after Prussia merged with the other German states to form the German Empire, in 1870. About 1877, he received a posting to Peking, but he declined the appointment and came, instead, to Britain and Wallasey.

This was the man who had spent his last 30 years in semi-isolation, squalor and poverty at Wallasey. When he died his assets amounted to the hut, a few sticks of furniture, the clothes he wore, and seven pence halfpenny in his pocket. According to the police, there was nothing among his many papers to reveal the identity of the person or persons who had sent Kreuger his allowance, and who might have helped to meet the costs of his funeral. He looked destined for a pauper's grave.

And then, something amazing happened. The local community's affection for their Hermit led to scores of Wallasey residents clubbing together to ensure that he received a decent send off. In the event, such was the sum raised that Frederick Kreuger's funeral, held on 13th March 1909, became something of a grand occasion, with the body carried in a magnificent coffin, drawn in a glass-sided hearse by four black-plumed horses and followed by a host of mourners.

Kreuger died, as he had lived, a man of mystery. Why, around the age of 30, had this highly-educated and gifted man abandoned a promising career and, with it, the cultured world in which he had moved? Why did he come to Britain, and – of all places – choose Wallasey as the site for his refuge? And, why the self-imposed loneliness and the attempt to shut out the world? No one knew. No one will ever know. Kreuger's mystery died with him, nearly a century ago, in a ramshackle little hut at Wallasey.

THE CONGLETON
CANNIBAL

In 1776 Congleton was the scene of a horrific murder with an almost equally horrific sequel. Most of the known facts are preserved in the records of the inquest on the victim.

About midday on Saturday, 23rd November, Newman Garside, a Congleton ribbon-maker and farmer, turned his cows out in a field located on the side of a shallow valley between the town and the tiny village of Astbury. A field that sloped down to the edge of a stream called 'Howty Brook'. Garside closed the gate behind him, and then walked down to check the fence which ran along the edge of the brook. As he was making his inspection, one of the two boys who were helping him, 13-year-old William Barratt, drew his attention to what looked like a woman's blue cloak in the water below them. Garside sent the boy down to have a closer look.

William pulled the garment out, and called that there was 'something bloody' underneath it.

His curiosity aroused, Garside crossed the wooden footbridge which connected his land to Priesty Fields, on the other side of the stream, with his other assistant (unnamed in the records). By the time they joined William, the boy had added a yellow gown to the cloak he had already retrieved. There were great bloodstain patches on its lining. Convinced that something was seriously amiss, Garside called and beckoned to two men he had seen working in a field further above him. The two, who were known to

Garside and his assistants as Humphrey Newton and John Beswick, hurried to join them.

After Garside had showed Newton and Beswick the wet and bloody garments and explained the circumstances, the three men and the boys set about a systematic search of the brook. They soon added a petticoat, a cap, a black ribbon and a woman's small bag to the gown and cloak on the bank. The bag held a half-eaten threepenny brown loaf, an old tobacco box, a pair of scissors, a thimble, two ballads [song sheets] and a sewing bag, containing needles, thread and related items.

Their next finds were grisly. Beswick discovered a woman's right arm, severed at the elbow, and a leg, cut off at the knee joint. They continued their search and found another arm and leg.

At that point, the boys were despatched to find the parish constable. During their absence, the men found a woman's breast and a clump of bowels.

The messengers returned with Parish Constable John Martin and a number of other locals who had caught wind of the matter from the boys. With the search party in the brook reinforced by the men among the new arrivals, what appeared to be the remainder of the victim's body – the head, the tongue, the neck and so on – was soon found. Collected together, these pathetic human remnants were laid in a nearby stable overnight.

The following day – Sunday – events moved quickly: the body was identified as that of 22-year-old Ann Smith, an itinerant ballad singer, and buried; the inquest on her death was launched; and, by nightfall, a man was under arrest, charged with her murder. The early arrest was the fruit of some remarkable detective work by Thomas Cordwell, a local weaver.

Until the Police Acts of the 19th century paved the way for the introduction of professional police forces, local parish constables were essentially part-time, amateur, officials, appointed by the local parish authority. That being so, it was normal for members of the local community to help the constable by taking a much more active part in the investigation of serious crimes than would be considered appropriate today.

Thomas Cordwell appears to have been endowed with all the personal qualities needed in a good police officer, and had he been born a century later, it seems likely he would have applied to join the county force, formed in 1856.

Early on the Sunday morning, Cordwell returned to the brook. Searching to make sure that all the evidence had been collected, he found a black ribbon. On the way home, he saw a certain Samuel Thorley talking to two other men. As he passed them, he heard Thorley claim that he first learned of the murder on the previous evening. In fact, he said it several times while Cordwell was still within earshot.

Thorley was well known – almost notorious – in the Congleton area as a simple-minded, and homeless, labouring man in his early fifties. From time to time, he worked for a local butcher, hacking animal carcasses into manageable chunks for his employer to trim into joints, and he was also a gravedigger at Astbury parish church. He was a big, morose man, with a temper so vile that locals treated him with extreme caution.

When Cordwell reached home, his wife told him that there were those who were openly saying that Sam Thorley had committed the murder. It seems to have been a conclusion based on the man's known character, and the fact that the body had been dismembered in a way that suggested the sort of basic skill that Thorley might have acquired by working for his butcher employer. Cordwell thought that they could well be right, and, with his own suspicions already stirred by Thorley's odd, repeated, insistence that he had known nothing of the crime until after the body had been found, he decided to investigate the possibility.

First, he called on a friend named Charles Butterworth. He told Butterworth of his suspicions and suggested that they should examine Thorley to see if they could find any bloodstains on him. Butterworth agreed and the two men then combed the area, looking for the suspect. They were, however, unable to find him, and Butterworth went home.

Cordwell was not so easily discouraged. He called on another friend, Thomas Elkin, to explain his suspicions. Elkin told him that on the previous afternoon, when he had been helping to scour the area around the murder spot, he had spotted bloodstains on a stile across a footpath that ran from Priesty Fields and past a certain Hannah Oakes' cottage. When Cordwell inspected the stile, he found that the bloodstains were still visible. Suddenly, as he looked at them, he was startled by a flash of insight. It was well known locally that Thorley occasionally slept rough in barns. It was also well known that he enjoyed eating raw animal meat. Was it possible that, in the seclusion of a local barn, he had tried human flesh?

He decided to organise a search of all the barns in the area to see if any additional evidence could be found. It then occurred to him that, before he returned to the town to do so, it might be as well to ask Hannah Oakes whether she had seen anything of Thorley – perhaps passing her cottage on the footpath. It proved to be the best move he could have made.

The elderly widow told Cordwell that Thorley had been lodging with her for the previous few days. When he asked whether there had been anything odd about Thorley's behaviour, the story she outlined heightened his forebodings.

She said that Thorley had turned up at about 8 pm on the previous Wednesday evening with wet feet, and with his apron full of meat. He explained that he had been walking through Priesty Fields along the brook when he had slipped and, to avoid falling full length into the stream, he had jumped and landed on his feet, in the water.

Asked about the meat, he said it was pork. He claimed that he had killed a pig for someone and had been given the meat as payment.

He threw the meat down on the table, and asked Hannah to boil some for him. She said she had refused because she had not liked the look of it. Thorley then placed it in the cold oven. The following evening her lodger had boiled some of the meat himself. He had started to eat it, but had been violently sick after only a few mouthfuls.

Thorley, she said, had left the house earlier that Sunday afternoon in an agitated state, only minutes before Cordwell had arrived, telling Hannah, 'I am going to my master's at Astbury to get my wage, and go to Leek, as they are laying the charge of murder on me.'

'What happened to the meat?' asked Cordwell.

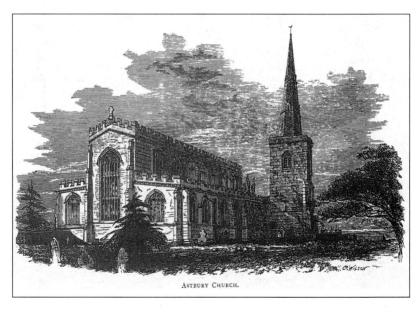

ASTBURY CHURCH.

Thorley's victim, Ann Smith, was buried at Astbury church on 24th November 1776.

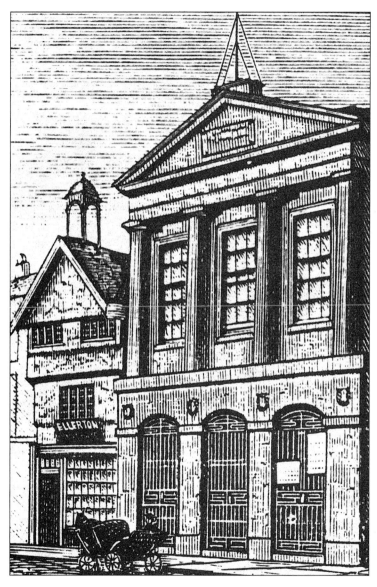

Sam Thorley was locked up in Congleton Old Town Hall on the night of 24th/25th November 1776, before he was transferred to prison at Chester. The building was demolished in 1864.

'It's here, in the back place,' replied the widow, and led the way into the kitchen. She took a tray out of the cold oven and set it down on the table. It was piled high with white meat. Even before he touched it, Cordwell must have known what it was, just short of certainty. He ran his hand over a piece, which he guessed to be the calf of a leg, and found it to be smooth and soft. 'I think it's a woman's flesh!' he declared.

'God forbid!' exclaimed Hannah. 'He told me it was pork.' For both of them, it must have been the stuff of nightmares.

The local surgeon, Charles Reade, later confirmed to the inquest jury that he had examined the flesh and established that it was, indeed, that of a woman.

Cordwell found Constable Martin outside Astbury churchyard questioning some of the crowd who had attended Ann Smith's funeral. After he had told him about the new – damning – evidence, Cordwell and Martin, joined by John Beswick, started to search for Thorley. Late that afternoon, they came across him at another house where he occasionally lodged, in School Lane, Astbury. Martin arrested him, and then the three of them escorted him to Congleton Town Hall, where he was locked in for the night. The following day he was transferred to Chester City gaol, to await trial at the next Chester Assizes.

After the inquest jury had returned a verdict of wilful murder against Samuel Thorley, the coroner's clerk would have sent the records on the case to the clerk to the Assizes.

On Thursday, 3rd April 1777, at Chester Assizes, Samuel Thorley was charged with the murder of Ann Smith. Unfortunately, the trial records no longer exist, and the newspaper reports of the time were – surprisingly for such a macabre case – somewhat brief. At no point, it seems, did Thorley provide a clear account of the events which led to the murder, or offer an explanation for his actions, or make any sort of plea in mitigation. Indeed, according to the newspapers, he exhibited complete unconcern and indifference to the events that were swirling about him, both before and during the trial. Discussion of his fate, it seems, did not detain the jury for long. He was found guilty, and sentenced to be hanged, with his body to be gibbeted afterwards on West Heath, near Congleton.

Thorley was executed at Boughton on Thursday, 10th April 1777. According to *The Chester Courant* of 15th April, he did not show the least remorse for the horrid and unparalleled crime he had committed, and behaved, on the whole, with the greatest unconcern and indifference.

On 11th May, in accordance with the second part of the sentence, Thorley's body was suspended from a gibbet on West Heath. A gibbet was a high wooden frame on which the bodies of executed criminals were, semi-permanently, exhibited near to the scene of their crimes, as warning to others who might be tempted into lawlessness. West Heath was chosen for Thorley's gibbet because it was the most prominent spot close to Priesty Fields.

While Sam Thorley's execution and gibbeting closed the matter as far as the Law was concerned, his death left a number of questions unanswered; or, at least, not answered satisfactorily. Why did Thorley kill Ann Smith? What was his motive? Why did he attempt to eat some of her flesh?

They were questions that only Thorley could have answered, and Sam Thorley, simple-minded, morose, and possessed of a volatile temper, was not an easy man to interrogate.

As far as the cannibalism is concerned, *The Manchester Mercury* of 15th April claimed that, on being questioned as to what could induce him to commit so ghastly a crime, he answered that, having frequently heard that human flesh resembled young pig in taste, curiosity prompted him to try, to see if it was true. It is, however, a report that lacks a certain measure of credibility in as much as *The Mercury* neglected to state the occasion on which Thorley was being questioned, and by whom, when he was alleged to have said it.

The murder remained a major topic of conversation and a source of material for writers in the Congleton area for a century and more. Prompted by the general ignorance of the details of the fatal encounter in Priesty Fields, a host of myths gathered about the known facts and merged with them. Over those years, a number of possible scenarios were proposed, but none of them was completely convincing. It does seem, however, that even the wildest flights of fancy did not visualise Sam Thorley as having killed Ann Smith to eat her. All of them agreed that the cannibalism was an afterthought.

By 1887, when Robert Head wrote his *Congleton, Past and Present*, the many versions of the murder had been merged into one, generally accepted, explanation of the crime. Head outlined it as follows, 'It will never be known what led to the horrible fate of Ann Smith. Thorley himself, in some interval of the stolid indifference with which he behaved after the event, let fall a sort of account of the matter to the effect that the woman met him and borrowed his pocket knife ... in order to cut some bread and cheese which she was carrying for her dinner [it will be remembered that a half-eaten brown loaf was found in one of the deceased's bag], and that having got it, she laughed at him and ran away with it. He followed her to the brook and took the knife from her and, in a rage, cut her throat, after which, in his fury, he committed the rest of the frightful excesses ...'

And there, the matter seems destined to rest for ever.

THE DEATH OF A
HAVE-A-GO HERO

Standing in the churchyard of St Peter's church, Prestbury, a fine altar tombstone marks the grave of William Wyatt, a local man, who died on 12th February 1848, from a gunshot wound received while assisting in the arrest of two itinerant footpads.

The first person in the area to be aware of the men, who were to reveal themselves as robbers, was James Williamson, the Special High Constable of Macclesfield, whose responsibilities included the parish of Prestbury. He was riding along the turnpike road from Macclesfield to Adlington Hall in Prestbury at about a quarter past three on the afternoon of 11th February 1848, when he overtook the two, walking in the direction of Adlington.

About a quarter of an hour later, the same two men passed a Macclesfield corn dealer, James Ernill, who was walking home along the road, in the opposite direction. After the two parties had passed each other, the duo turned and followed Ernill for a few hundred yards. Suddenly, one of them, later identified as William Bates, aged 30, rushed up to Ernill, and grabbed him by the waistcoat, presented a pistol to his forehead, and said, in a broad Irish accent, 'Damn and blast your bloody eyes, give up your watch and your purse this minute, or you're a dead man.'

The other man, later identified as John Mawdesley, aged 26, put a pistol to Ernill's ear and, in similar language, also spoken with an Irish accent, told him that if he did not do as he was told he would blow his head off.

Ernill answered, 'If that's what you intend you'll find me rougher than you think.'

At that, Mawdesley knocked Ernill down with the butt end of his pistol, and both men proceeded to kick him. They then allowed him to get to his feet, and, again pressing the muzzles of their pistols to his head, made the same demands. When he, again, refused to hand over his watch and purse, they knocked him down a second time and set about kicking him once more.

On the ground, Ernill remembered that, a short way back along the road, he had passed a man working on a bridge, and, as soon as the robbers allowed him to scramble to his feet again, he ducked under their pistols and ran towards the bridge, calling out for help. Scattering sand on the bridge, to give horses' hooves a better purchase, Thomas Ardern heard the commotion. Looking up, he saw a dishevelled and hatless, but otherwise well-dressed, man pursued by two

William Wyatt's tombstone in Prestbury churchyard.

scruffy individuals who were brandishing pistols. As he started forwards, the pursuers overtook their quarry. There was a scuffle, and all three fell into a ditch. Ardern arrived at the spot as Bates and Mawdesley were in the act of scrambling out.

The two robbers untangled themselves and slowly backed away, pointing their pistols at Ardern, and making bloodcurdling threats about their intentions if he dared to follow them. When they had retreated for ten or fifteen yards, they turned and ran. In the meantime, Ernill, filthy and bloody, scrambled out of the ditch. A quick check revealed that, in the struggle, the footpads had snatched his watch-chain, two keys, and two seals.

Ernill and Ardern followed the footpads at a safe distance as far as the next house – Pole House Farm – where they were joined by a man named Albert Mitchell, who raised the cry of 'Stop, thief'. As they continued to follow the robbers they were joined by others, who left their various workaday tasks to join the pursuit – some bringing sticks, or the tools of their occupations, such as hammers or spades, to use as weapons. From time to time, Bates turned round and threatened to fire on the pursuers. Their response was to stop, but they did not fall back. When the robbers turned and ran again, the pursuers continued to follow them. The chase reached the bank of the Macclesfield Canal, which was where the pursuit was joined by the brothers William and Thomas Wyatt, who worked at the nearby Shrigley Quarry.

The footpads started to cross the canal bridge, but paused at the top, from where they pointed four pistols over the parapet at their pursuers – by that time numbering about 20 – and threatened to shoot.

Still followed by the pack, Bates and Mawdesley fled from the bridge, across a field, and into a wood, called Blake Hey Wood, at Adlington, where they turned at bay.

Surrounded by the members of the impromptu posse, Bates went down on his knees, placed his hat on the ground, and shouted: 'I swear, by the faith of Jesus and Saint Patrick. Oh yes, once; Oh yes, twice; and here goes the third time; and now I swear by Almighty God that the first man that comes forward I'll shoot him.'

'Nay, lads, tha wunna,' said 41-year-old William Wyatt, starting towards him, closely followed by his brother, who looked set on grabbing Mawdesley. Immediately, Bates shot William and Thomas with the two pistols he held, one in each hand.

William fell to his knees, but although Thomas was thrown backwards by the impact of the bullet he managed to stay on his feet.

Mawdesley, too, fired a pistol, but the ball flew wide of its target – whoever that was. Immediately, the uninjured pursuers closed with the footpads and, after a violent struggle, subdued them.

James Ernill, who seems to have assumed a sort of command because of his socially superior station, then despatched a man to Adlington Hall to let the Lord of the Manor, Richard Legh, know of the incident and of the need for medical assistance for the two wounded brothers.

Legh sent four servants and a wagon to bring the casualties to the Hall, and another to request the attendance of two local medical men, a Doctor Vaux and a surgeon, Mr Newbold. Fortuitously, James Williamson, the Special High Constable of Macclesfield, had also completed his journey to the Hall by that time. Responding to the news of the incident, he set off to meet the prisoners. On reaching them he handcuffed each of the footpads to one of the escorts, and then took the four horse pistols the robbers had been carrying from the escorts who had seized them.

Back at the Hall, he found that Bates was semi-conscious from his share of the bruising that the pair had collected by resisting arrest, and was in no condition to answer questions. Only after he had been revived with some brandy and water and allowed to rest for half an hour, was he able

The Special High Constable of Macclesfield, James Williamson, interrogated and charged the footpads in the Great Hall of Adlington Hall on 11th February 1848.

to comprehend the situation he and Mawdesley were in. A search of the prisoners revealed that Bates had about his person: a powder flask filled with gunpowder, eight bullets, a quantity of percussion caps and some wadding. Mawdesley had thirteen bullets, eight percussion caps and some powder in his possession.

When Bates had recovered sufficiently to understand what was said, Williamson told them both that they were under arrest, charged with robbing a man on the highway, and shooting two others who had been endeavouring to take them into custody. Bates replied that they had not robbed Ernill; they had merely told him that they were penniless, and asked him for financial help. When

Williamson asked them where they had acquired the pistols, they both claimed that they were old family pieces.

In the meantime, the two Wyatt brothers had been brought to the Hall and the medical men had also arrived. An examination revealed that the ball had entered William Wyatt's body under the left breast, and it had come out towards the lower part of the back – a finding that left little cause for optimism. His brother had been more fortunate: the bullet had passed through his shoulder, and there seemed no reason to doubt his prospects of making a full recovery.

Because there were grave fears for William Wyatt's life, Richard Legh, as a magistrate, took his deposition without delay. In that deposition, William stated that it was Bates who shot him.

Bates and Mawdesley spent that night in Macclesfield Town lock-up. By the time they were transferred to Chester Castle, the following day, 12th February, Bates was facing a murder charge, and Mawdesley a charge of being an accessory to murder. William Wyatt had died early that morning, leaving a widow and seven children, one of whom was just a week old.

Their trial began on 14th April and lasted two days. All of those personally involved in the incident and its aftermath testified, and so damning was their evidence that the jury was able to reach a 'Guilty' verdict on both men after a mere ten minutes.

When the judge, Mr Justice Williams, asked the prisoners if they had anything to say as to why sentence of death should not be passed upon them, Mawdesley exclaimed that he had been forced into crime by poverty. He said that the man for whom he had been working in Birmingham had not paid him his wages, and he had eaten hardly anything for days before the murder was committed. He commented that it was a cruel thing that he should suffer death for the sins of his hard-hearted master.

The judge was unmoved. He donned the black cap and pronounced the death sentence on both men.

At that, Bates called out, 'Well, my Lord, I'll die cheerfully.'

The executions were set for the 28th April.

A week before the appointed date, Mawdesley's sentence was commuted to transportation for life. A day before the execution, Bates and Mawdesley did something to redeem themselves by confessing, before a magistrate and the governor of Chester Castle gaol, that they had carried out a highway robbery near Manchester, for which two other men, Patrick O'Brian and Michael Conolly, were in Kirkdale gaol under sentence of transportation for 15 years. They were able to describe their victim on that occasion, the Reverend Mr Gormon, the time and circumstances of the robbery, and the items they had stolen – a watch, a watch-chain and a number of seals. They were also able to provide details of the person who had bought the watch from them for £7. Although their confessions were made separately, they tallied in every detail. Accepted as genuine, their declarations were forwarded to the Home Office, and the innocent men were released three weeks later.

Came the day of execution. The gallows had been erected on Castle Square, Chester, and the usual crowd gathered from early in the morning. Bates was led out to the scaffold at a few minutes before eight o'clock. Amongst others, his bearing impressed the observer from the *Chester Chronicle*, who reported that the condemned man stood quietly on the trap, remained calm while the noose was adjusted, and, when that was accomplished, he called to Heaven for mercy.

The bolt was withdrawn, and he fell to his death.

The main details of William Wyatt's death are inscribed on his tombstone at Prestbury. Also recorded are the facts that the tomb was erected by public subscription; the sum of £1,000 was raised for the benefit of William's wife and children; that £400 was raised for Thomas Wyatt, who was wounded in the same incident; and that a further sum of £170 was distributed among the others who assisted in the arrest of the footpads. Including the cost of the altar tomb, the total raised must have been the better part of £2,000 – an astonishing sum for a time when most working people would have been lucky to be earning 15 shillings a week. Although the inscription states that the cash was raised by public subscription, it is certain that little could have been donated by the ordinary folk of the parish, and a second inscription on the stone leaves no doubts about the source from which most of it came: 'Long may the poor of England have wisdom to discern the right, and stout hands to maintain it. Long may the rich have liberal hearts to sympathise with the weak, and to reward the deserving. Give God the praise.'

Reading between the lines, it seems that the fund was one way in which those with most to lose tried to ensure the support of those with least to lose. It can, of course, equally be regarded as having been a generous gesture by some wealthy local residents, who had no legal obligation to do anything. And the awards from the fund were certainly a more realistic and acceptable recognition of the posse's bravery than medals and certificates would have been.

THE GAMEKEEPER AND THE POACHER

Although John Bebbington was murdered a century and a half ago, the crime still lives on in the folk memory of the neighbouring villages of Tilstone Fearnall and Alpraham.

At five o'clock on Friday morning, 17th April 1857, farm worker Thomas Chesters, hurrying to get to work on time, cut across the corner of a wheatfield at Tilstone Fearnall. As he did so, he spotted a body, lying on the ground and close to a gap in a hedge. He stopped, and went over to it. He saw that it was lying with its limbs akimbo, and with the right leg hanging over a ditch. A shotgun lay nearby. Looking closely, he recognised local gamekeeper John Bebbington. He took hold of an arm in an attempt to ascertain whether Bebbington was still alive or not – he might possibly have been just unconscious. Deciding that Bebbington really was dead, Chesters rushed to tell his employer, tenant farmer John Sheen, of his discovery.

Sheen immediately hurried to the spot where the body was lying, with two of his men. After he had examined the body and found a large gunshot wound in the left side, he inspected the gun and established that it had not been fired. He then instructed his men to move the body to the nearby house of a Mr Hall. As soon as he had done so, he went to inform the Lord of the Manor, Edwin Corbett, of his gamekeeper's death. Corbett responded by despatching one man to inform the senior local police officer of the crime, and another to request the attendance of surgeon John Croxton-Foulkes, of Bunbury.

When Mr Croxton-Foulkes examined the body, he discovered that he could insert four fingers into the wound in Bebbington's side. The following day he conducted a full post-mortem, and found that the shot had passed through the victim's left lung and shattered his heart, causing instant death.

Superintendent Francis McDermott of the Eddisbury Division of the county received the information of Bebbington's death at about seven in the morning, and arrived at the scene at about nine o'clock. Accompanied by Constable John Kearns, he first went to Mr Hall's house to inspect the body, and then, guided by John Sheen, he went on to the scene of the murder. Near the gap in the hedge, McDermott found a quantity of clean partridge feathers and some wadding from shotgun cartridges. He also noted two sets of footmarks, one of which, he realised, must have been made by Bebbington. He sent Kearns to Mr Hall's house to collect one of the gamekeeper's boots. When the constable returned, McDermott compared the boot with both sets of footprints, and found that it matched one trail of impressions, which came down from the hedgeside and into the gap. That being so, he deduced that the other set of footprints had been made by the murderer.

He and Kearns set off to follow the trail of footprints. Although it disappeared in places where their quarry had walked over grass or hard ground, they were able to pick it up again without too much difficulty. It led them on and into the township of Alpraham, then into Sandy Lane, and finally, at about 10 o'clock, to the cottage home of 47-year-old John Blagg, a shoemaker and notorious poacher.

They found Blagg standing in the yard, inspecting a piece of leather. According to McDermott, giving testimony at the subsequent trial, he 'changed countenance' when he saw the officers.

The superintendent greeted him, 'John, you are suspected of taking away the life of John Bebbington.'

Blagg replied, 'It is not so.' In McDermott's statement to the court, when he asked him at what time he had risen on the Thursday, Blagg said, 'Between six and seven o'clock.'

After questioning Blagg about his movements, he and Kearns searched the cottage, and confiscated Blagg's shotgun. On McDermott's orders, Kearns then took one of the suspect's boots, and walked back along the trail of footprints, stopping to press the boot into the ground at various points alongside the existing impressions. In doing so, he found that the print produced, with its distinctive pattern of nails, exactly matched those which had made the trail.

With the evidence of the footprint trail, bolstered by his knowledge of the poacher's past criminal record and of a long-standing personal animosity between Blagg and the gamekeeper, McDermott arrested Blagg on a charge of murdering Bebbington. The prisoner was held in Tarporley lock-up for the night before being taken to Chester Castle on the following day.

Almost incredibly, with all this activity, no one had thought to tell Bebbington's widow of his death: not his employer, Edwin Corbett, and not even the local vicar, Henry Harding, who would certainly have been notified. Nobody. At Blagg's trial, Catherine Bebbington testified that she had last seen her husband alive at three am on Thursday, 16th April, when he went out on his early-morning rounds. She had been alarmed when he did not return for his breakfast. The *Chester Chronicle* did not mention the extent of her enquiries over the next two days, but it did report her as saying that the first she knew of his death was when his body was brought home on the Saturday, after the post-mortem. It was clear, from her testimony, that her husband's corpse must have laid in the field for something like 24 hours before Chesters discovered it.

The delay in finding the body temporarily misled McDermott. Although he stated in his testimony at the trial that, during his initial interview with Blagg on Friday, 17th April, he questioned him about his movements on the Thursday morning, he could not possibly have done so, because did not then know that the murder had taken place on the Thursday. He would have assumed that it had occurred that same Friday morning, and questioned Blagg accordingly. No doubt, when he realised his mistake, he found an early opportunity to question Blagg again, in order to correct his record, but it would not have been the sort of blunder he would have admitted to in court, or anywhere else.

The trial commenced at Chester on Friday, 7th August 1857. According to the *Chester Chronicle*, it opened with John Blagg pleading 'Not guilty' in a loud, distinct voice. If there were those in the packed courtroom who believed that he was innocent, they must have felt their conviction crumbling before the mass of circumstantial evidence produced by the prosecution. Witness after witness contributed to a picture of a man who hated Bebbington, and who was in the vicinity of the murder scene at the time when the crime was probably committed.

Among those who testified to the animosity between Blagg and Bebbington was a certain Peter Smith, who stated that, some two years previously, the prisoner had told him that Bebbington had knocked him down, taken his gun from him and abused him. Blagg had then added that if Bebbington ever tried to take his gun away again, he would shoot him. Ann Williams, who was described as a servant at the Travellers' Rest public house, said that she had often heard Blagg curse Edwin Corbett, the Lord of the Manor, and say he would 'put a thorn in Bebbington's gap'.

Among the witnesses whose collective evidence disproved Blagg's statement that he rose between six and seven o'clock on the morning of 16th April was James Vickers, a labourer who lodged with the Blaggs. Vickers testified that when he rose, between four and five o'clock, he found that the door was unbolted and that Blagg's hat and boots were missing. He went to work close to the house, and he saw Blagg coming home at about five o'clock.

Farm labourer William Williams was in his own garden at a quarter to five in the morning, when heard a gunshot. A few seconds later, he heard another. The reports came from the direction where Bebbington was found. He saw Blagg from 10 to 15 minutes after the shots were fired, near a by-road leading down to the spot where the body was found.

In addition to confirming the testimony of the other witnesses which had established the fact that Blagg was up and out of the house before five, blacksmith George Whalley's statement placed him close to the scene of the crime. He saw Blagg a little after five o'clock in Wood's Lane, walking from the direction where Bebbington's body was found. He turned into the adjacent turnpike road and hurried along in the direction of his house.

Telling the jury that no significance could be attached to the fact that none of the witnesses saw Blagg carrying a gun on the morning of the murder, prosecuting counsel James Macintyre showed them Blagg's coat, with its deep inside pockets, specifically designed to hold a concealed shotgun, broken down into two or three parts.

Added to the mass of evidence offered by the many other witnesses – among them the police with their analysis of the footprint trail, the ballistics experts and Croxton-Foulkes, the surgeon who conducted the post-mortem – these statements built a prosecution case that was about as sound as any circumstantial case could be.

Even so, Blagg's defending counsel, Frederick Brandt, did his best to discredit it. He, unsuccessfully, suggested to those witnesses who saw Blagg on the morning of the murder that they might, by mistake, have been recollecting the events of the Wednesday morning instead of the Thursday. He asked the jury if they did not think it strange that, although it had been established that Bebbington had been killed by an Eley-manufactured cartridge, the police had failed to find any similar cartridges in the possession of the prisoner. As for the footprint trail, he pointed out that there were two nails in the centre of the heels of Blagg's boots which were not reflected in any of the plaster impressions that the police had taken. Further, only one boot had been used to make the comparison with the prints – the implication being that the other boot might well have offered more differences from the corresponding footprint than just the two additional nails. He tried hard, but his efforts were not good enough.

It took the jury just 25 minutes to reach a 'Guilty' verdict. The judge, Mr Justice Crowder, obviously shared their certainty, because he passed the death sentence with the minimum of comment.

According to the *Chester Chronicle*, the prisoner heard the sentence unmoved, and throughout the trial he gazed sullenly round on the crowded audience.

There were, however, those, drawn from several levels of society, who were still set on trying to save Blagg. While it seems clear that there were a number of motives, it is equally clear they did not include respect and personal affection for Blagg. Although he was married, John Blagg was something of a loner. At the Travellers' Rest he would sit for hours without speaking a word, but in a morose, dogged manner he would remain drinking, taking no notice of anyone, and apparently attempting to live within himself.

It may be that one major element in the campaign to save Blagg was launched shortly after his arrest. Only a few days later, and long before the shoemaker had been found guilty, the Lord of Alpraham Manor, James Tollemache, ordered the eviction of Blagg's wife and 4-year-old child from their cottage. A blatant and spiteful abuse of manorial power, it precipitated something approaching a class war in the township. Some residents, it seemed, vowed openly that they would not testify at the trial. To which, apparently, Tollemache let it be known that he would evict any of his tenants who refused to appear. The clandestinely rebellious element in the village then responded to that by threatening to beat up anyone who was prepared to testify – indeed one witness, Charles Vickers, was delayed on his way to the trial by a gang who threatened him.

Immediately after the trial, Thomas Jones, solicitor for the defence, and Andrew Johnson, of Tarporley, drew up a petition to the Home Secretary asking for a reprieve. The petition did not claim that Blagg was innocent, but, instead, it focused on the danger of capital punishment based on circumstantial evidence. It was sent to the Home Secretary, Sir George Grey, by the prison chaplain, with a covering letter:

'Chester Castle   August 21st 1857

Sir,
    At the request of the solicitor of John Blagg, now lying under sentence of death in this prison, I have the honour to forward their accompanying petition, which has been numerously signed by citizens of Chester.
    Although I do not myself hold the peculiar opinions of the memorialists, I most cordially join with them in the abstract plea for mercy on behalf of a suffering fellow creature, and very thankful, indeed, should I be, if, after careful consideration of the case, which its importance demands, you should be pleased to recommend her most gracious Majesty to spare the life of the unhappy man it is my painful duty to have in charge.
    The execution is, at present, fixed for Friday next, and I await your reply with considerable anxiety, as it is important for the wretched man to know the result of this appeal as early as possible.

I have the honour to be, Sir, Your most obedient, humble, servant,
J.M. Kilner, Chaplain.'

Frederick Brandt, Blagg's counsel, also made a last effort to save Blagg by writing to Sir George Grey:

'... I do not feel that I should have discharged my duty to this unfortunate man were I not to state to you the opinion which I have formed (after most anxious and painful consideration of the evidence adduced at the trial) of the real facts of the case. Two shots were heard, one following the other at an interval of only a few seconds: a quantity of partridge feathers were found close to the spot where the body of the deceased was discovered, and I feel convinced that Blagg, having first shot a bird, the keeper (the deceased) suddenly appeared from behind the hedge, and that, without a moment's thought, the prisoner fired the other barrel at him, and killed him instantaneously; but that he went out in the first instance for the purpose of committing murder, I cannot believe. Now, if this view be a correct one, the offence would surely be manslaughter, not murder, even though Blagg was in the act of doing what was illegal. I have delayed this application until so late a period in the expectation that some application would be made to me in the matter by the friends of the convict. No such application has reached me; I have, therefore, ventured to lay this short statement before you with the object of relieving my conscience of a heavy responsibility, and trust that the importance of the subject may be taken as my apology for my presumption in thus addressing you.'

Meanwhile, a search made in the midden at Blagg's cottage by a number of Alpraham villagers was said to have yielded a pair of old boots which, it was claimed, were the boots Blagg had been wearing on the Thursday morning of the murder. These, it was pointed out, had only 16 nails in each boot, as opposed to the 22 in the boots tested by the police. It was, however, a claim that failed to impress Superintendent McDermott, who retorted that the boots had certainly not been in the midden when he and Kearns had searched the cottage.

The Home Secretary rejected the appeals of both Brandt and the petitioners for clemency. In what was, substantially, the same letter to each of them, a civil servant replied:

'... I am to acquaint you that, after full consideration of the evidence given at the trial, and of the report of the Judge upon the case, Sir George Grey is quite satisfied that the verdict was right, and that there is no ground which would justify him in recommending an interference with due course of law.'

Within a day of the arrival of the news at Alpraham, a rumour was circulating to the effect that the appeals had been doomed to fail even before they were sent. According to the word on the village street, the local Lord of the Manor, James Tollemache, who was a Member of Parliament, had spoken personally and privately to the Home Secretary, and tilted the balance against Blagg.

The execution was set for Friday, 28th August 1857.

The Deputy Sheriff of Cheshire, Richard Bordessa, seems to have shared the widespread uneasiness about the execution. On the preceding night he made the prisoner as comfortable as possible, in the circumstances, by moving him from the bleak condemned cell to a room with a good fire, and then he spent many hours talking to him.

After the execution, he reported that, during their conversation, Blagg alleged that much of the evidence against him had been falsified. He said that he had not been

For much of the 19th century, public executions were carried out on Chester Castle Square. It was here that John Blagg was hanged on 28th August 1857. Others who died here included William Bates (28th April 1848), and Alice Hewitt (28th December 1863).

near the spot of the murder for three weeks. He also said that the boots alleged to have been worn by him were taken from him, and that they were used to make the trail of prints. These statements, according to Bordessa, were made with great earnestness.

Came the morning. Came the time. The crowd that gathered on Chester Castle Square to watch the execution – described by the *Chester Chronicle* as '... not as numerous as on previous occasions' – saw John Blagg meet his death with courage and dignity.

Commenting on the case, the *Chronicle* observed, 'No confession was made by the prisoner, and therefore certain doubts as to the guilt of the executed man may exist.'

Indeed. In fact, there is a legend in Alpraham to the effect that, many years later, an unnamed local who emigrated to

Canada confessed to the murder on his deathbed. He stated that, having a personal grudge against John Bebbington, he decided to shoot him. Believing that Blagg would almost certainly be the prime suspect in such a murder, he had 'borrowed' his boots and gun, and used them to commit the murder.

John Bebbington is buried in Tilstone Fearnall churchyard.

THE STOCKPORT POISONER

To Alice Hewitt (also known as 'Holt') belongs the unenviable distinction of being the last woman to be publicly hanged in Britain. Her crime was matricide.

In February 1863, at the start of the series of events which were to lead to her execution, 27-year-old Alice Hewitt, a widow, lived in Stockport, with her lover, George Holt, whose surname she had adopted. Their home was shared by Alice's 51-year-old mother, Mary Bailey, also a widow. The three of them occupied the front two rooms of the four-roomed house, while they sub-let the back two rooms to a married couple, George and Ann Bailey. Although the two Bailey families shared a surname (a surname which was, of course, daughter Alice's maiden name) they were not related.

Mary Bailey was physically disabled, and unable to work. Her only income was parish relief, and she was, therefore, partly dependent on her daughter and George Holt for financial and practical support. Although Holt was in regular work and, according to his testimony at the trial, paid most of his weekly sixteen shillings wage toward housekeeping expenses, and although he and Alice must have made a profit from sub-letting part of the house, they were often in the sort of difficulties that obliged Alice to visit a pawnbroker. These financial difficulties she appears to have blamed on the cost of meeting Mary's needs, and, added to the physical efforts needed to cater for her disabled mother's daily demands, they created a festering sense of resentment in Alice's soul. And the knowledge that she was pregnant offered the prospect of even more physical and financial stress when the baby arrived. Increasingly, she saw her mother as a burden, and her feelings were transformed into action when Mary fell ill in mid-February 1863.

On the 18th, Alice managed to obtain an order for her mother to be visited by the Union (workhouse) assistant surgeon, Walter Barker, who diagnosed chronic bronchitis. Presumably disappointed by his assurances that the illness was unlikely to prove fatal, she then contrived to secure a visit from the parish doctor, Dr Thomas Raynor – possibly in the hope that he would declare Mary's illness to be terminal. In the event, he, too, diagnosed bronchitis. Both medical men continued to visit Mary at various times over the next five or six weeks – that is, until her death at the end of March – each of them apparently unaware of the other's visits. With them, they brought the medicines they had prescribed for Mary's illness – medicines which Alice promptly threw away as soon as the doctor concerned had left the house.

At some time shortly after the doctors' first visits, it must have occurred to Alice that, while her mother's death would relieve some of the financial and physical pressure on her, it would not bring any immediate and direct financial gain. If, however, she could manage to insure Mary's life, and then murder her without being detected, she would be able to claim the death benefit. Towards that end, she contacted Samuel Garlick, a schoolteacher, who was also a sub-agent for the Wesleyan and General Insurance Society.

In response to her enquiries, Garlick told her that, if her mother passed the necessary medical examination, Alice would be able to insure her life for £25.16s at a premium of sixpence a week. Alice knew that there was not the slightest chance that Mary would pass the examination and be accepted by the insurance society, but if the problem gave her any cause for reflection it was not for long. Knowing that Garlick had never met Mary, she conceived the idea of persuading someone to impersonate her mother at the examination.

First, she asked her tenant and friend, Ann Bailey, to play the role, but she was met with a firm refusal. She then wrote to another friend, Elizabeth Wells, at Didsbury. Elizabeth received the letter on 5th March, and travelled to Stockport the following day. At the trial, Elizabeth's explanation for her subsequent actions, to the effect that Alice had told her that 'anyone will do', seems to reveal her as being particularly naive. Be that as it may, the fact remains that she agreed to pose as Mary during an interview with Peter Scarlett, a chief agent for the insurance society, and then, afterwards, before a doctor acting for the society, '... as long as I'm doing no harm.' It can only be supposed that Elizabeth was, or looked, considerably older than her friend Alice, to pass as her mother.

The ruse was successful. On 23rd March, Scarlett delivered a note to Alice's home stating that the proposal had been accepted, a note which, with the payment by Alice of a fortnight's premium, brought the policy into force.

Alice did not waste time. On the morning of 25th March 1863, she went to a druggist's shop in Heaton Lane, Stockport. She asked druggist Henley Davenport for three pennyworth of arsenic, but he refused to serve her until she brought a witness aged over 21. That afternoon she asked Ann Bailey to accompany her to the shop, explaining that, in order to buy arsenic, she needed an adult witness. When Ann asked her why she wanted the poison, Alice replied, 'To kill vermin, lice, cockroaches and such.' They went to the druggist's where, after they had both signed the poisons book, Davenport served Alice with the arsenic.

On the evening of 26th February, Alice dissolved the poison in a cup of brandy, and gave it to her mother. When Mary complained about the grounds in the bottom of the beaker, Alice told her to drink every last drop because she had paid sevenpence for the brandy.

By the next morning Mary was dead. A few days later she was buried at the Wesleyan Chapel at Stockport.

'Well, Ann,' Alice remarked callously, and somewhat injudiciously, to Ann Bailey, 'I am very glad my mother has died. I have all my clothes fast [ie at the pawnbroker's] and I wanted money to relieve [redeem] them. If she had not died, it would have been God-help us. George would have leathered me.' On 8th April Peter Scarlett paid Alice the £25.16s for which she had insured her mother, less the cost of the mourning clothes, which he had already supplied to Alice and George Holt.

Alice did not have long to enjoy the money. It is not clear exactly what prompted the murder investigation, but, six months later, the *Chester Chronicle* was to record that, at Alice's trial, prosecuting counsel Richard Smith simply stated, '… it came to the ears of the insurance society that a fraud had been committed on them.'

On 12th June 1863 Mary Bailey's corpse was exhumed. A post-mortem was performed by Dr William Raynor, who found the equivalent of 160 grains of what he suspected was crystallised arsenic in the body – the fatal dose being something under two grains. By way of a quick test, Raynor folded two crystals into a paste, made from a small piece of bread, and fed it to a pigeon, which died within forty minutes. He then subjected some of the crystals to a number of standard scientific tests, which confirmed that they were, indeed, arsenic.

In the course of the subsequent murder inquiry, Sergeant William Walker, of the recently-formed Cheshire Constabulary, searched Alice's home and confiscated the cup which had held the fatal drink. Dr Raynor inspected the inside surface of the cup very closely, and noticed that it was marred by a very deep crack. When he tested the vessel for the presence of arsenic, he discovered that, although it had been scalded out and used several times since the murder, he was able to detect traces of the poison – a finding that he attributed to their lodging in the crack.

Alice was arrested and gaoled at Chester Castle. She should have appeared at the Summer Assizes, but her trial was postponed until December because she was pregnant. When it eventually took place, starting on 9th December 1863 and lasting for two days, a series of witnesses testified to a series of events that left no room for doubt about her guilt. They included: Sergeant Walker; Ann Bailey; Elizabeth

The courtroom at Chester Castle, where Alice Hewitt was sentenced to death on 10th December 1863.

Wells; druggist Henley Davenport; insurance society officials Peter Scarlett and Samuel Garlick; a neighbour, Catherine Ryan; and Alice's live-in lover George Holt. Despite a clever and impassioned closing speech by defending counsel James Swetenham, so clear-cut was the evidence that the jury returned after just half an hour to deliver a 'Guilty' verdict.

Immediately, Alice collapsed in the dock, wailing piteously, 'My baby! Oh, my poor baby!' – a sight which wrung a great groan from the packed public gallery. It seems that, throughout the hearing, Alice had somehow excited general sympathy in the court – perhaps it was something to do with her appearance and demeanor. It may also have been partly due to popular revulsion at the image that George Holt unconsciously projected of himself from the witness box. Although he was able to establish with little difficulty that he had not been involved in the murder, he then went further and made every effort to distance himself from Alice. He admitted that he had not visited her once during the long six months she had spent in prison, nor even provided her with any other sort of support in the shape, for example, of letters, cash or extra food – nothing. Furthermore, he had shown no interest in his new baby son.

The only person to visit Alice in prison had been Holt's uncle, John Holt, who had also looked after the baby, and who later adopted him.

Whatever the roots of the sympathy, it had obviously affected the jury (all male, as the law of the time required) which added a strong recommendation for mercy to its verdict.

Unfortunately for Alice, this general mood of sympathy did not touch the judge, Mr Justice Evans. Commenting that, in his opinion, poisoning was the most heinous method of murder, because there was no defence against it, he told her she should not place too much hope on the jury's recommendation for mercy.

As soon as the judge retired, the gallery turned on George Holt. Jeers, catcalls and threats flew thick and fast, and there was a surge towards him, which the court police contained with difficulty. There were signs that the crowd was about to turn into a mob. So ugly was their mood that the police whisked Holt out of the courtroom, and into temporary protective custody.

The jury's plea for clemency fell on deaf ears. Early on the morning of 28th December 1863, a crowd, estimated to be of about a thousand in number, gathered on Castle Square, Chester, to witness the execution. At eight o'clock Alice Hewitt was led out to the gallows, which stood in front of the Castle. As she reached the steps of the scaffold her courage failed her, and the escorting prison warders were obliged to half-carry, half-drag her up them. On the platform she fell to her knees, and wailed, 'The Lord have mercy on me.'

To add to the horror of the scene, the execution was bungled. When hangman Albert Calcraft pulled the bolt, the trap only partly fell. Then when, after some confusion, it was freed and pulled down, the fall was not sufficient to break Alice's neck, and she dangled, alive and writhing, for two or three minutes, while the rope strangled her to death.

IN SEARCH OF THE CHESHIRE CAT

In 1983 I was fortunate enough to acquire a working notebook of the late Richard Leatham, the Cheshire writer, naturalist, broadcaster, and local historian. Bought at an attic sale, the notebook is actually a loose-leaf quarto-sized file covering the years 1949 to 1951. Among the many projects that Leatham recorded was his attempt to unravel the mystery of the Cheshire Cat, and to use the results of his quest in a book to be called 'Out and About in Cheshire'. He knew that the Cheshire Cat existed in popular county usage long before Daresbury man Charles Lutwidge Dodgson – otherwise Lewis Carroll – conferred international fame on the creature by including it in the pages of his *Alice in Wonderland*. There is, however, no agreement about the identity of the original, or why it should grin, or why it should keep appearing and disappearing.

It was during the spring and summer of 1949 that Richard Leatham made a number of trips about the county in an attempt to collect the evidence which might allow him to solve the great Cheshire Cat mystery.

He started his quest on Wednesday, 11th May, at Chester Central Library, which, in those days, was located in St John Street. To eke out his petrol (still rationed after the War), he made the journey from his Hooton home to the city on the train. In the weeks that followed, he managed to hoard enough petrol to use his ancient bullnosed Morris car to make the other trips involved in the search.

Leatham visited the library in an attempt to acquaint himself with the existing known data about the Cheshire Cat, as a basis from which to launch his research. In the event, he discovered, as he had suspected, that there was a marked lack of hard facts about the creature. Indeed, he learned that there is not even a legend involving the animal – merely the notion of a grinning cat that lives in Cheshire. The problem was further compounded by an abundance of widely-differing theories about the origins of the notion, none of which can claim a pre-eminent credibility. One school of thought holds that the idea dates from the Cornovii people who lived in parts of what is now Cheshire in Roman times, and whose tribal symbol was the cat. Another maintains that the myth of the Cheshire Cat was born during medieval times when the local cheese was commonly sold in edible cat-shaped pieces. Yet another traces it to John Catherall, who lived in the early 14th century and whose crest was a cat. As Chief Forester of Mara, Catherall was invested with the power of life and death within his jurisdiction. He is remembered for his savage treatment of poachers and thieves, and for the terrible grin that contorted his face when he was enraged. And there are many other theories, all equally plausible, but none provable. So many, in fact, that Leatham came to see his original project of unravelling the mystery of the original Cheshire Cat as hopeless. Instead, he decided that he would attempt the somewhat more realistic objective of discovering the source of Dodgson/Carroll's inspiration for his particular Cheshire Cat.

Back at home that evening, he opened his copy of *Alice* to refresh his memory of Carroll's cat. He found that it appears in Chapter VI, 'Pig and Pepper', acting as a sort of link between the Duchess's kitchen and the Mad Hatter's tea party, and that it possessed three main characteristics: it lived in Cheshire; it grinned; and it had the habit of suddenly appearing and disappearing.

From a copy of *Victoria Through the Looking Glass*, the life of Lewis Carroll by F.B. Lennon, borrowed from his

The Cheshire Cat talks to Alice in a scene visualised by Lewis Carroll's first illustrator, John Tenniel.

local library, Leatham discovered that Charles Lutwidge Dodgson was born at the old parsonage at Newton-by-Daresbury on 27th January 1832, five years after his father, also named Charles Dodgson, had been inducted as vicar of Daresbury. In addition, he learned that the Dodgsons had relatives scattered about various parts of Cheshire.

These facts reminded him of one particular set of related theories that he had encountered at Chester Library. Theories which prompted him to wonder whether Dodgson/Carroll had gleaned the idea for his Cheshire Cat from one of the many representations of cats to be seen in public places throughout the county, and which he may have seen as he travelled with his family to visit his relations. He may also have heard of the claims made for some of these creatures as being the original Cheshire Cat. These felines include the second-century Romano-Celtic rock carving of a cat-faced goddess on Bidston Hill, overlooking Birkenhead, and the lion crest of the Egertons which appeared on the signs of all the inns belonging to that great land-owning family.

It seemed to Leatham, however, that the cat representations with which the devout Dodgsons would be most familiar would be those that appeared in the churches they visited. Accordingly, he decided to tour some of the churches concerned to assess the merits of the various cat representations to be seen there for himself.

During the course of that summer of 1949, he visited Tilston church, located in the Broxton Hills, which had connections with the Catherall family – including John Catherall of the sinister grin. There he saw a window containing a few fragments of ancient glass, and, in the centre, a cat. High above the west window of Grappenhall church, he saw a carving in black stone of a snarling cat, which locals claim as the original Cheshire Cat. It was, however, in Pott Shrigley church, on the eastern fringes of the county, that Leatham discovered the representation that

Photograph of the cat grotesque at Pott Shrigley church, often claimed to be the original Cheshire Cat.

he found to be the most convincing as a possible inspiration for Dodgson/Carroll's character. Inside the church, under the chancel arch and built into the wall, there is a stone grotesque representing a grinning cat.

The octogenarian vicar of the parish, the Rev Carl Waldemar Aslachsen, told him that there were many others who favoured the claims of that particular carving, including the members of the Archaeological Society who had visited the church in 1922.

So far so good. Leatham had found a cat that grinned persuasively, but what about Dodgson/Carroll's cat's habit of appearing and disappearing? It was a characteristic that distinguished it from all the traditional claimants to the title of 'The Cheshire Cat'. The vicar had a suggestion and a theory about that. Standing to the south of Macclesfield,

Detail from the Lewis Carroll Memorial Window at Daresbury parish church. The Cheshire Cat peers out from oak tree foliage between the Knave and the Queen of Hearts.

and just inside the Cheshire-Staffordshire border, a hill known as 'The Cloud' incorporates a sheer rock face known as the 'Cat Stones'. Seen from a certain point, the feature has a natural image of a giant cat's face, formed from time-etched cracks and curves. There is, however, no sign of a grin. If the observer takes a pace to the left or right, the cat disappears; a pace back again, and it reappears. The Rev Aslachsen thought that the young Dodgson could have seen the Cat Stones, and achieved his own special Cheshire Cat by adding the 'Now you see it; now you don't' phenomenon to the widely-known notion of a grinning feline.

Leatham found the vicar's ideas appealing. So much so that he would have pressed on from Pott Shrigley to visit the Cat Stones if, by doing so, he had not risked the possibility of running out of (rationed) petrol. As it was, he decided that he would inspect the stones at the earliest opportunity. In the meantime, he noted in his workbook a comment that he was unlikely to encounter a better explanation.

The next cat trip he took was on Thursday, 28th July, when he went to Daresbury as a sort of pilgrimage to Dodgson's birthplace. He knew, of course, that the house had burnt down in 1883, but he went to the site anyway. There he found that only the well remained. He then went on to the church to inspect the Lewis Carroll stained-glass window, installed in 1932, to mark the centenary of Charles Ludwidge Dodgson/Lewis Carroll's birth. The window portrays Carroll with Alice, and many of the characters from the *Alice* books, including the Cheshire Cat, which peers out from oak tree foliage between the Knave and the Queen of Hearts.

In the event, Leatham does not seem to have inspected the Cat Stones, and if the proposed book was written, it was never published.

Gaol Break

The Brenans – two brothers and a cousin – were highwaymen. More than that, they were highwaymen with some style. Contemporary accounts described them as 'handsome'; they wore fine clothes; they rode thoroughbred horses; and they employed servants. Among everyday folk they commanded a reputation for courage, dash and audacity. Unfortunately, most of the records concerning their professional career and background appear to have been lost. From those fragments that have survived, however, it has been possible to assemble something close to a full account of one of their most notable exploits. Documents housed at the Irish Record Office in Dublin record that the Brenans were arrested in Chester, imprisoned in the city's Northgate Prison, and made their escape from that gaol. There are, however, unexplained details in the episode that are likely to remain mysteries for ever.

The Authorities were jubilant when, in late October 1683, they learned that the Brenan Gang – brothers 'Little' James and Patrick and their cousin 'Tall' James – had been seized in Bridge Street, Chester, and were safely lodged in the city's gaol.

Before their first arrest, two months previously, they had ranged over south-west Ireland for some three years robbing many of the King's wealthier subjects of a total estimated at more than £12,000 in cash. It is, perhaps, interesting to note that they had not been charged with murder, or any other violent crime; violence, it seems, was, for them, a last resort. Tried, convicted and sentenced to death for robbery, they had been brought out to be hanged, but, at the last minute, had been rescued from the gallows and the hands of the hangman.

Proclaimed outlaws, with rewards on their heads, in Ireland, they were pursued by bands of armed men. The hunt became so warm that they decided to leave Ireland, and try their luck across the water. It was a bad decision. Just days after their arrival at Chester, one of their former victims, Alexander Marshall, recognised them and denounced them in the street. It seems that, at the time, it was the practice for all the able-bodied men in the vicinity of a suspected criminal who was denounced to help in his arrest – possibly in the hope of a reward. That being so, a number of stalwarts rushed to grab the Brenans. One of the gang – the records do not state which – tried to draw his sword but he was overpowered before the blade was clear of its scabbard.

The Mayor of Chester, Alderman Peter Edwards, passed the good news of the Brenans' arrest to the Duke of Ormonde, then Lord Lieutenant of Ireland, at his home in St James's Square, London. The Duke thanked the Mayor, and asked him to 'have a careful eye to them'.

On behalf of the Mayor, Matthew Anderton JP wrote to the Duke of Ormonde's secretary (the spelling has been modernised and archaic words and phrases replaced by appropriate modern equivalents):

Dear Sir   Chester, 20th October 1683

The enclosed will inform you of the apprehension yesterday of some outlawed Irish highwaymen. I thought it to be my duty to send the news to you, to be communicated to his Grace, my Lord Lieutenant of Ireland. We are holding the robbers' four thoroughbred horses and a bill of exchange for £50.8.0d and are detaining the men in our common gaol.

A number of local men helped to arrest them at the risk of their lives. Fortunately, only one was wounded, in grabbing the blade of a sword which one of the rogues started to draw. They are dressed in the height of fashion, and it is thought that they have a considerable sum of money, which is currently in the possession of an accomplice, who is somewhere in North Wales. We have sent agents out to look him.

These men shipped their horses from Dublin in a vessel bound for Mostyn. They followed in another ship, and landed at Beaumaris. They came to Chester, and were recognised and denounced by Mr Alexander Marshall.

I hope his Grace will order those who helped with the arrest of these men to be generously rewarded, because they deserve to be well paid considering the danger they ran in doing so.

On 23rd October, the Duke of Ormonde replied to the Mayor:

'I note that you have the Brenans, who robbed Alexander Marshall, in Ireland, and were for that and other crimes outlawed there, in gaol. I thank you for your good work in arresting these criminals, and ask you to keep them in custody until I decide the best way to return them to Ireland. In the meantime, their horses, goods, and money should be kept safe, and the bill of exchange for fifty pounds found with them sent to me, so we can find out who it was drawn upon and who drew the bill, which could well help us to make another arrest. If these men have been proclaimed outlaws in Ireland, as Alexander Marshall claims, a reward will have been offered in the proclamation, which, when the robbers have been convicted will be paid to those who helped to arrest them.'

The Chief Justice of Ireland, John Keating, wrote to James Clarke, steward to the Duke of Ormonde's household, on 1st November 1683, but it is not clear from where he was writing:

'I have already given you an account of the robbery committed by the Brenans and their accomplices at Mr Bolton's house of Brazile.

His Excellency (the Duke of Ormonde, Lord Lieutenant) was so furious about it that, because the judges of the King's Bench were all out working in their circuits, he ordered me personally to organise the search for the thieves. The Brenans were caught and sentenced, but, when they were brought out to be executed, they made their escape from the gallows in a way that I do not feel inclined to describe here. No doubt, you will hear the story later.

Last Thursday, His Grace (the Duke of Ormonde) was notified that the Brenans had been arrested at Chester, and that they had in their possession some bills of exchange. I am told that they are extremely rich, and that if they could bribe their way to a pardon, or to the freedom to leave the country, even it cost £2,000 or £3,000 (equivalent to £200,000 or so in 2002) they would not hesitate to do so.

I complained to the Duke that the Mayor of Chester is making too much difficulty about sending the Brenans back to Ireland without a warrant from the King, as soon as I arrived in this town. [Dublin? Chester? London?]'

The level of excitement that the arrest of the Brenans generated in the Authorities involved may be gauged by the dates of the letters. With the dismally slow means of inland communication that prevailed during the late 17th century, it seems reasonable to suppose that for a letter despatched from Chester on the 20th of the month to be answered at London, two hundred miles away, on the 23rd, it must have been carried by a special couriers – a hard-riding relay of horsemen.

Chief Justice Keating's letter is particularly interesting. His refusal to reveal the details of the Brenans' escape from the gallows in Ireland was very obviously rooted in the personal humiliation inflicted on him by the coup. A second interesting point is Keating's eagerness to have the Brenans back in his jurisdiction, where he can exact his revenge on them – an impatience which is obvious in his anger at the Mayor's insistence on the production of the correct warrant before he will release the prisoners for transfer back to Ireland. Here is a prominent member of the judiciary advocating an illegal action!

On 19th October 1683 the Brenans were confined in the city gaol, housed in the massive medieval Northgate. On 2nd November – the day after Chief Justice Keating wrote his letter to the Duke's steward – they broke out.

The gaoler, Richard Wright, gave his version of the escape in a statement, taken down by the Mayor's secretary. According to Wright, the three Brenans arrived at the gaol, escorted by 'several' constables. He searched them in the presence of the constables, and took the papers and money they had about them into his keeping. He then shackled their legs. After that, he made sure that they were shackled every day, and, at night, he shackled them to their beds, and took away their day clothes until the following day.

About 8 pm on 2nd November, the three highwaymen – still in irons – Thomas Greene, a prisoner in gaol for debt, and a certain Thomas Clarke had all eaten supper with himself and his wife Frances in 'the Lower Room'. During the meal the Brenans were very peaceable and quiet.

At about 9 pm, Thomas Clarke stood up, made his farewells, and left. About half an hour after he left Thomas Greene remarked, 'I should think Mr. Clarke will be home by now.' At that (Tall) James Brenan spoke in Irish to the other two. Suddenly, daggers appeared in all three Brenans' hands.

(Little) James, who was sitting next to Wright, thrust his blade at the gaoler's throat, but he, reacting swiftly, raised his arm and took the point on his wrist. Wright called out 'Murder' and his wife screamed.

Seizing Wright by the coat, his assailant snarled, 'God damn me. If you speak another word, I'll cut your throat.' He threw Wright to the floor, and pinned him down with the dagger at his throat. He told the gaoler that if he called out again he would kill him.

Wright said that he would not call out.

At the same time, (Tall) James attacked Thomas Greene. His attempt to cut his victim's throat also failed, but, in making the attempt, he slashed Greene on his face. As his part in the simultaneous attack, Patrick threw Frances Wright to the floor and threatened to murder her if she screamed again.

With their victims subdued, the Brenans allowed all three to stand up, swearing them all to silence, under pain of death.

Patrick Brenan went to the cupboard where Wright kept his keys and his weapons. He returned with a sword, an extra dagger and the keys to the shackles. He unlocked his own and his comrades' shackles, and secured a set of the irons on Greene's legs. He then unsheathed the sword and, with the point at Wright's chest, he told the gaoler again that if he called out he was as good as dead. Searching the gaoler's pockets, he found the keys to both the cells and the outer doors.

(Little) James then told Wright that there was a prisoner in gaol for debt, called William Browne, who they intended to take with them when they made their escape, and that if the gaoler did not agree they would kill him. Browne's cell had not yet been locked for the night, and it became obvious that he was expecting the summons to join the Brenans because, when Patrick called him, he was standing at the top of the stairs. As soon as Browne joined the Brenans, Patrick warned Wright, Frances and Greene, yet again, not to make any noise. All the escapers then trooped to the top of the stairs, where Patrick unlocked the outside door. He blew out the candle he was holding, opened the door and led the others into the night, taking the keys with them.

As soon as they left, Wright rushed upstairs to check that all the other debtor prisoners were secure. Reassured on that point, he raced to the outside door and shouted, 'Murder! Murder!'

At which, according to Wright, the escapers returned and would have murdered himself, his wife and Greene, if he had not had the presence of mind to bolt the door on the inside.

Soon after the escapers had given up the attempt to get at Wright and company and had left a second time, Alderman John Wilme arrived at the gaol. When Wright told him about the escape, Wilme set about organising the pursuit of the gang.

Although Richard Wright's statement was signed by Thomas Greene and Frances Wright, as being a true account of the events leading to the escape, it leaves a number of important questions unanswered.

The first is, obviously, how did the Brenans acquire the daggers, which became the key to their break-out? At its simplest, it could have been a matter of someone smuggling the three daggers into the gaol and passing them to the Brenans. Could it be that it was done by some visitor? Possibly a visitor to William Browne, who then passed the weapons on to the highwaymen? Debtor prisoners had more freedom within the gaol than criminal convicts, and it would have been comparatively easy for Browne to give the weapons to the Brenans. Was it a service done on condition that they would take Browne with them when they broke out?

Until prison accommodation was built at the remodelled Chester Castle, about 1800, the city gaol was housed in the massive medieval Northgate (demolished 1808). It was from this prison that the Brenans made their escape on 2nd November 1683.

Or was it more far-reaching than that? Could it have been an inside job? Such a possibility is suggested by the fact that there are a number of points in the statement that do not ring quite true. Was the gaoler involved? Interestingly, Wright's statement (again, rendered into modern English) concludes: 'And further, I emphasise that none of the three men, neither by themselves nor any person or persons whatsoever on their behalf, did, at any time, offer or promise me any bribe to let them escape, and that they really did make their escape from the gaol in the way I have described, and that, during the time they were in gaol, I did not receive any money from them, except that which I found on them when they arrived at the gaol, and which I took into my keeping, and of which I gave the mayor a proper account.'

If that was so, why did both the all-action Brenans who attacked Wright and Greene manage to bungle their murder attempts? Why did they fail to follow up their initial attacks, and leave their victims with no more than what seem to have been superficial wounds? Why did they then fall mildly back on their victims' undertaking not to call out, instead of permanently silencing them? After all, their lives were at stake. Why did they shackle Greene, but leave the gaoler and his wife unshackled? If they jibbed at murder, the obvious course would surely have been to shackle and gag all three. Did the daggers actually exist, or did Wright take the precaution of making sure that he held the only available weapons? And, if that was so, were the injuries suffered by himself and Greene self-inflicted? And is it really likely that, having started to create some distance between themselves and the prison, the escapers would have stopped, and turned back to exact their vengeance on Wright and company? Or, is it more likely that the gaoler fabricated that particular point as an excuse for his having kept the door shut, and by doing so, given himself a good excuse for the delay in raising the alarm – which afforded the escapers extra valuable time? All questions which seem to suggest the existence of an escape plot.

If there was a plot, could the Mayor himself, Peter Edwards, have been involved? In his letter to the Duke of Ormonde's steward, Chief Justice Keating mentioned his fears that the Brenans would be able to draw on their very considerable resources to offer the sort of bribes that could tempt many of those responsible for their safe custody. Big enough, perhaps, to tempt even a prominent civic dignitary?

Having been warned that the Brenans were dangerous and resourceful, why did the Mayor fail to strengthen the watch over them with additional gaolers? And, since it would be reasonable to suppose that he would want them out of his gaol and his city as quickly as possible, why did he delay their departure by insisting on the letter of the law? Did he engineer the delay to create enough time for the other participants in the plot to play their parts? Unfortunately, the surviving records do not provide any answers to these questions. The extent and character of the plot – if there was a plot – remain a mystery.

DOCTOR DEATH

Before the trial it would have been hard to imagine anyone looking less like a serial killer than Dr Harold Frederick Shipman. A smallish, middle-aged, grey-bearded and balding man, Shipman was a familiar and respected figure about the former mill town of Hyde and the surrounding area. The high esteem in which he was held was reflected in the impressive total of some 3,100 patients who were registered with his one-doctor practice. Elderly women, in particular, found the GP's gentle and solicitous manner reassuring. Yet, following a trial which had lasted for 57 days, Shipman was convicted of murdering 15 women. Worse – much worse – it seemed likely that those 15 women represented only a small percentage of Shipman's victims. Speaking on television after the trial, the local coroner, John Pollard, said, 'A total of about another 130 cases are being investigated by the police relating to the past three or four years. If you extend that over the period of his professional life, it is possible to say, on a statistical basis, that 1,300 to 1,500 people were victims.'

Detective Superintendent Bernard Postles, who had supervised the investigation, could find no other motive for the murders than personal satisfaction. He came to the conclusion that Shipman was simply a serial killer who enjoyed what he did. 'He wants to control situations,' he said. 'He likes to have control over life and death.'

Shipman's victims were all patients, were all middle-aged or elderly, and they were all at his mercy. With one exception – a death in the surgery – they were all killed at

Harold Shipman.

home, with a few muttered words of comfort and an injection of diamorphine – the pharmacists' name for heroin. Time after time, Shipman was the last person to see his victims alive, but he escaped suspicion under the cloak of professional respectability, and his insistence that there was no need for a post-mortem examination.

The first victim with whose murder Shipman was charged was 81-year-old widow Marie West, who died on 6th March 1995. When Shipman arrived to visit her he was unaware that her friend had just left the living room to go to the bathroom. At the trial, the friend recalled that when she returned to the kitchen, she heard the doctor talking quietly to Mrs West, followed by a silence. Shipman walked into the kitchen and, surprised to find someone there, said Mrs West had collapsed and died. He said 'She's gone' and made no attempt to revive her. He did not contact the emergency services.

The next victim with whose death Shipman was charged was Irene Turner, a 67-year-old widow, who died on 11th July 1996. Complaining of a heavy cold, she had arranged for the doctor to call. After he left her house, Shipman told a neighbour that he had arranged for her to be admitted to hospital, but the neighbour found her lying dead on her bed. The police investigation was to discover that there was no record of a call made from the house to the hospital that day.

Lizzie Adams was a sprightly 77-year-old widow, who had given up her part-time job as a dance teacher only a year before her death on 28th February 1997. She had been taking antibiotics, which did not agree with her, and had telephoned the surgery asking for Shipman to make a home visit. A close friend found her front door open, and Shipman inside. He told her that Mrs Adams was ill and that he had telephoned for an ambulance. He then declared, 'She's gone. I'd better cancel the ambulance.' Again, the police investigation was to reveal that no call had been made from the house to the ambulance service.

Jean Lilley, aged 58, was married to a long-distance lorry driver. She was complaining of a bad cold just before she died on 25th April 1997. A neighbour saw the doctor walking away from her house. Inside, she found Mrs Lilley's cold, dead body. When Shipman returned, the friend accused him of knowing his patient was dead before he left, which he denied.

Ivy Lomas, a 63-year-old widow, was the only one of Shipman's victims included in the charges to be killed at his surgery in Hyde High Street. Twenty minutes after she was shown into his treatment room on 29th May 1997, Shipman emerged to say he was having problems with his electrocardiogram machine. He then left Mrs Lomas in the treatment room while he attended to three other patients. He told his staff that, when he returned to the treatment room, he found she had died.

Muriel Grimshaw, a widow aged 67, was found dead by her daughter on 15th July 1997. Her diary showed that she had been expecting a visit from Shipman the previous day.

Shipman's next victim was 67-year-old Marie Quinn, also a widow. On 24th November 1997 she phoned her son, John. In court, John Quinn described his mother as having been in good spirits when they talked. At 8.30 pm Shipman told one of Mrs Quinn's friends that she had died two hours after phoning him at the surgery to say that she had apparently suffered a stroke and was partly paralysed. The police investigation – two years later – was to discover that there was no record of a call from the house to the surgery that day.

On the morning of 9th December 1997, Laura Wagstaff, an 81-year-old widow, had appeared her normal, cheerful self. That afternoon a neighbour saw Shipman arrive at her house. Thirty minutes later, the doctor knocked on the neighbour's door to say that Mrs Wagstaff was dead.

The following day 49-year-old Bianka Ponfret, the youngest of Shipman's victims, was found dead in her living room with the television blaring and a half-empty cup of coffee by her side. When the doctor was summoned he said that he had called earlier to treat the German-born divorcee for chest pains, and had diagnosed heart attacks. The police investigation was to reveal that Shipman had created a false medical history of chest pains and angina for her.

Norah Nuttall, 64, another widow living alone, was overweight and complained of feeling unwell before visiting the doctor on 26th January 1998. When her son went to her house later that day, Shipman answered the door. His mother was slumped in a chair. Shipman told him, 'She seems to have taken a turn for the worse.' He felt for a pulse, and then turned to say that he would cancel the ambulance because it would not be needed now. She was cremated a week later. Yet again, the police investigation was to find that no request had been made for an ambulance.

The following month Shipman murdered two women in ten days. On 9th February a neighbour found Pamela Hillier, 67, another widow, lying on her back in a bedroom. Shipman told family members that he had treated her for high blood pressure, but she had obviously died of a massive stroke. She was cremated a week later.

Spinster Maureen Ward, 57, had given up her job as a college lecturer after she discovered she had breast cancer in 1996. She was looking forward to a Caribbean holiday when she died on 18th February 1998. Shipman told the warden of her sheltered accommodation block that she had died from a brain tumour. Like Pamela Hillier, she was cremated.

Not every Hyde resident was oblivious to the sinister events that were unfolding under their noses. In spring 1998, local undertaker Deborah Bambroffe told Dr Susan Booth, a GP at another surgery, that she was uneasy about the fact that many of Shipman's elderly women patients seemed to be dying at a much faster rate than those registered with the other surgeries in the town. Dr Booth, too, had her own misgivings about the situation. She was concerned by the number of times she had been asked to be the second signatory on Shipman's cremation certificates, and by the fact that, in each case, it seemed that Shipman had found the body or had been nearby when the body was discovered. That being so, she contacted the local coroner, John Pollard. She told him, 'I have a horrid feeling that something may be dramatically wrong.'

The coroner contacted Chief Superintendent David Sykes, who briefed a detective inspector to conduct discreet inquiries into the matter. The detective examined the printed records lodged with the local health authority by Shipman, looking for signs that the cause of death given for his patients was not consistent with their treatment. He did not find any, and came to the conclusion that claims that Shipman had always been close by at the time of death were unfounded. Almost incredibly given the nature of the inquiry, he did not discover that Shipman had covered his tracks by changing his computer records. All that being so, the police decided that they did not have enough hard evidence with which to confront the much-respected Dr Shipman and, after six weeks, they dropped the investigation.

Shipman murdered Winifred Mellor on 11th May, Joan Melia on 12th June and Kathleen Grundy on 24th June 1998.

It was in the murder of 82-year-old Kathleen Grundy that Shipman finally overreached himself. For once, not satisfied with the murder itself, he tried his hand at forgery. In doing so, he was to discover that he was not nearly as clever as he thought he was.

Friends described Mrs Grundy, a former Mayoress of Hyde, as being well and in good spirits on the morning of her death but they became alarmed when she failed to turn up at a pensioners' luncheon club which she helped to run.

They found her lying, apparently dead, on a sofa at her nearby home, and called Shipman. He carried out a cursory examination, and then advised the friends to contact a local firm of solicitors who, he said, he believed acted for Mrs Grundy. Kathleen Grundy was buried in Hyde Cemetery.

On 25th June an envelope arrived at a firm of local solicitors, Hamilton Ward, containing a document purporting to be the last will and testament of Kathleen Grundy of Loughrigg Cottage, 79 Joel Lane, Gee Cross. It was written on a manual typewriter, badly spaced and with a missing letter. It read: 'I give all my estate, money, and house to my doctor. My family are not in need, and I want to reward him for all the care he has given to me and to the people of Hyde. He is sensible enough to handle any problems this may cause him. My doctor is Dr H.F. Shipman, 21 Market Street, Hyde, Cheshire. SL14 2AF.' It was signed 'K. Grundy' in a spidery handwriting, and purported to be witnessed by a C. Hutchinson and a P. Spencer. A letter enclosed with the will, and written on the same typewriter, read: 'I think it is clear in intent. I wish Dr Shipman to benefit by having my estate, but if he dies, or cannot accept it, then the estate goes to my daughter. I would like you to be the executor of the will. I intend to make an appointment to discuss this.'

The letter, again apparently signed by 'K. Grundy', bemused staff at Hamilton Ward, who were experienced in probate matters, but had never dealt with Mrs Grundy. Their misgivings deepened when, four days later, another letter arrived, seemingly written on the same typewriter, stating: 'Dear Sir, I regret to inform you that Mrs. K. Grundy of 79 Joel Lane, Hyde, died last week. I understand that she lodged a will with you, as I, as a friend, typed it out for her. Her daughter is at the address, and you can contact her there. Yours sincerely, S. Smith.'

Mrs. Grundy's daughter, Angela Woodruff, a solicitor who lived in Warwickshire, had returned to Hyde to settle her mother's affairs. Knowing that her mother had made a will leaving her entire estate – estimated to be worth some £386,400 – to herself and her family, Mrs Woodruff was stunned when Hamilton Ward informed her of the existence of a later will.

The moment she looked at the new will, she knew it could not be genuine. Giving evidence at the trial, she was to say, 'As soon as I received a copy of the will and the letter, I was very uneasy and confused: the signature did not look right. The concept of my mother signing a document like that is inconceivable.'

Over the next month, Mrs Woodruff contacted the purported witnesses to the will, Claire Hutchinson and Paul Spencer, and discovered that they had been unsure about what they were signing for Shipman. Speaking on television after the trial, Mrs Woodruff, said, 'We had our suspicions, but we couldn't believe what we were thinking. After we had seen Paul Spencer we began to think that Dr Shipman had killed my mother, but it was very difficult to believe. Dr Shipman was a doctor, and we knew my mother liked and respected him. Everyone trusts their doctor, so for us to believe that the doctor had possibly forged a will and possibly killed my mother was a huge gap to cross. I'm sure it must have been a huge gap for the police as well.'

Back at her home in Warwickshire, Mrs Woodruff continued to wrestle with the problem. Finally, on 24th July, with her doubts overcome, Angela Woodruff walked into Warwickshire Police Headquarters, where she spoke to a senior officer. Three days later a fax arrived at Stalybridge Police Station, near Hyde, to set in train a series of events that was to land Shipman in the dock. Detective Superintendent Bernard Postles said, after the trial, 'Without Mrs Woodruff there would not have been a case against Dr Shipman.'

Police began by duplicating Mrs Woodruff's work. They discovered that Mrs Grundy's signature had been forged, and that, as Angela Woodruff had already discovered, the witnesses to the will had not been clear about what they had been signing. It emerged that the signatories were patients of Shipman, who had been plucked at random from the waiting room on Tuesday, 9th June. Significantly, one of Shipman's fingerprints was found on the bottom left-hand corner of the letter that had arrived at Hamilton Ward's with the will.

On 1st August 1998 police searched Shipman's surgery and discovered that the doctor held a huge stockpile of diamorphine, amounting to no fewer than 1,500 fatal doses. In addition, they confiscated a typewriter, which an examination showed had been used to type the contested documents.

That night police exhumed Mrs Grundy's body from Hyde Cemetery, and, during the following September, October and December, they carried out a further 11 exhumations. Tissue samples taken from the bodies were tested at the Forensic Science Laboratory at Chorley, and, in every case, were found to contain fatal quantities of diamorphine. As a check, hair samples were sent to Hans Sachs at the University of Munich. Professor Sachs was able to show that, again in every case, diamorphine had been administered close to the time of death.

Not that Superintendent Postles waited for all the tests to be completed. By October, he had decided that the police had a case that was sound enough to charge Shipman with murder and fraud. Senior officers had also learned enough about the man to settle on the tactics they would adopt at the initial interrogation. They had come to assess Shipman as an arrogant man, with an inflated idea of his own importance and intellect. That being so, Superintendent Postles was persuaded that a low-ranking woman, who Shipman would regard as his intellectual inferior, would be the best sort of officer to rend the cloak of lies he had donned to conceal his guilt.

Police investigations led to several bodies being exhumed from local cemetries.

Accordingly, no sooner had Shipman had been formally arrested by an inspector at Ashton-under-Lyne Police Station, on the afternoon of 5th October 1998, than he was handed over to two junior officers. Shipman, supported by his solicitor Anne Ball, found himself confronted across the interview room table by Detective Sergeant Mark Wareing and Detective Constable Marie Snitynski. It was Constable Snitynski who asked most of the questions.

As the officers steadily and remorselessly cut holes into the GP's explanations for the deaths of his patients, Shipman became less and less assertive. Finally, he broke down in tears. He was allowed time alone with his solicitor, and she reported that he had fallen to his knees, with tears streaming down his face, and that he was in no condition to continue.

Detective Chief Inspector Mike Williams, who helped to lead the investigation, later recalled: 'It was a deliberate ploy. I think it wrong-footed him. I believe he thought he was important enough to warrant the inspector. Having to answer the questions from a woman detective constable was even more demeaning. It showed in the inflection of his voice.'

On medical grounds, the police were never allowed to interview Shipman again. Their case had to be constructed on a foundation of circumstantial and scientific evidence. In the event, it proved to be more than enough. On 4th October 1999, Harold Frederick Shipman stood in the dock at Preston Crown Court facing 15 charges of murder and one of fraud. He pleaded 'Not guilty' to all of them.

On 31st January 2000 the jury announced their 'Guilty' verdict on all counts. After castigating Shipman at some length for what he called '... these wicked, wicked crimes', Mr Justice Forbes passed 15 life sentences for the murders, and a sentence of four years for forging Kathleen Grundy's will. Passing the sentences, he said: 'Harold Frederick Shipman, I have come to the firm conclusion the crimes you now stand convicted of are so heinous that in your case life must mean life. My recommendation will be that you spend the rest of your days in prison.'

That was not, however, the official end of the matter. A public inquiry into Shipman's multiple murders was established in January 2001 under the chairmanship of Dame Janet Smith. On 19th July 2002, it published an interim report, which included a finding that Shipman had murdered at least 215 of his patients, and may have been responsible for another 45. That being so, Harold Frederick Shipman has become the most prolific serial killer in British criminal history, with the number of his victims exceeding, by a wide margin, the 160 of the previous holder of that terrible distinction, Sweeney Todd 'The Demon Barber of Fleet Street', who was executed in 1802.

A PROPHECY FULFILLED

The date was 20th February 1954. 'The only way I'll ever come back to you is in a box,' 24-year-old Marie Bradshaw screamed at the husband she had deserted a month earlier. Her words were to prove eerily prophetic.

George and Marie Bradshaw had been married in 1948. Since their wedding they had lived at Alfred Street in Bury, Lancashire, where two children, a girl and a boy, were born to them. By mid-1953, however, their marriage was in difficulties, occasioned by George's interest in another woman. Marie decided to retaliate in kind. At about Christmastime in 1953, she took 23-year-old Milton Taylor home, and introduced him to her husband as a 'friend'. Like George, Milton Taylor earned his living as a labourer.

Early in January 1954 George and Marie quarrelled over Taylor, and George left the house. When he returned, on 20th of January, he found his wife and Taylor in bed together. There was a furious altercation which did not, however, become violent. That time it was Marie and Taylor who left the house.

From the postcards that Marie sent to their children, George discovered that his wife and Taylor were living at Crewe. On 20th February 1954, he went to the flat in Underwood Lane, Crewe, which Marie was sharing with Taylor. Told by the landlady that the couple were out, he went looking for them in the town. He encountered them in Queen's Park, and there, in public, he pleaded with his wife to return home, for the sake of the children.

Queen's Park, Crewe, where George Bradshaw confronted his runaway wife, Marie, and her lover, Milton Taylor, on 20th February 1954. (Collection of Paul Michell)

Marie told him that she was expecting a baby, and that she thought Taylor was the father. George replied that if she would only return to their own children, he and Marie could bring up the baby as if it were theirs.

At that, Taylor, who had stood silently by to that point, said that he wanted to see the baby when it was born because it was his.

Ignoring Taylor, George repeated his plea to his wife. It was then that Marie made her strange statement about only returning to him in a box. Realising that he could not persuade Marie to return to him, George caught the train back to Bury.

From what Taylor was to say later, when he and Marie went back to the flat, the landlady, who lived in the same building as they did, insisted that they should pack and leave immediately. They caught the last bus of the day to

Worleston, on the outskirts of Nantwich, and then decided to spend the night in an isolated farm hut, just off the Middlewich road, which they found to be open.

At about 10 am the following morning, 21st February, Taylor called on farm worker John Lee Mann, who was lodging at an agricultural hostel in Park Road, Nantwich. He was agitated and weeping. 'John,' he said, 'I'm in trouble. I have killed Marie. I have strangled her.' And he held out his blood-covered hands.

After Mann had questioned his friend, to satisfy himself that he really was serious, he persuaded Taylor to surrender to the police.

They went to Nantwich Police Station, where Taylor told Desk Sergeant T.S. Shone, 'I want to give myself up. I've killed a woman.' He said that, at about 8.50 am that morning, he had killed Mrs Bradshaw by strangling her with his tie. 'She got on my nerves. She would not let me sleep, so I strangled her.' Remarkably, by that time there was no sign of the tears and tremours that Mann had seen; Taylor appeared to be perfectly composed. Indeed, the duty officers were astonished by his cool demeanor. So much so that they experienced some difficulty in believing him. At last, partly convinced, Sergeant Shone and Inspector H.A. Murray went to the hut. There they found Marie's body lying, fully clothed, on a stack of bags of artificial fertiliser. It was covered with a white mackintosh. A reef-knotted necktie was secured tightly round the neck, and the face was covered with a red handkerchief, bearing – irony of ironies – a pattern of good luck tokens, including horse shoes, black cats and shamrocks. Finding the body to be still warm, the officers tried artificial respiration, but without success.

They returned to the police station, where, at 4.30 pm, Sergeant Shone charged Milton Taylor with the murder. Cautioned, Taylor replied, 'I have nothing to say.'

When the trial opened at Chester Assizes on 2nd June 1954, Taylor pleaded 'Not guilty'. His counsel, Edmund

Davies QC, did not challenge the facts of the case; instead he concentrated on the state of Taylor's mind at the time of the murder. He maintained that Taylor did not fully understand the seriousness of his actions. To support that argument he called on Dr Isaac Frost, Consultant Psychiatrist to the Liverpool Regional Hospital Board, attached to the Deva Hospital, Chester, as an expert witness.

Dr Frost described how, during an interview, Taylor had 'Smiled in a fatuous and irrelevant way, not in keeping with his surroundings or the position in which he found himself.' Referring to certain non-verbal intelligence tests, Dr Frost said that Taylor's score placed him in the mental age group of eleven and a half years, which meant that he was a certifiably feeble-minded person.

Asked by Mr Edmund Davies what had been the prisoner's attitude to the murder charge, Dr Frost quoted Taylor as saying, 'I strangled somebody, sometime in February. I wanted to. Just felt like it. She didn't upset me. I got satisfaction. Just felt better when I did it with a tie. When I want to do a thing, I do it, whatever the consequences. If I felt like it I would do it to anybody else. I think anybody should strangle anybody, if they feel like it. It would be right from their point of view. The way I look at it, I was quite right to do it. I don't feel sad or sorry; quite happy as a matter of fact.'

Dr Frost said Taylor agreed with him that other people would think such a thing was wrong. He also said he knew it was against the law. The doctor reported that Taylor had suffered inflammation of the brain following vaccination. Such a disease of the brain could, in his opinion, 'lead to disease of the mind'. He believed that on February 21st Taylor was labouring under a defect of reason from a disease of the mind, and that he did not know the nature of what he was doing, or that it was wrong.

Called by the prosecution, Dr F.H. Brisby, Principal Medical Officer, HM Prison, Liverpool, said he found no history of mental disorder in Taylor's family. He had found nothing to indicate that Taylor had, at any time, suffered from any mental disorder, or to support the opinion that he was suffering from brain inflammation.

Dr A.V. McKenzie, Medical Officer for HM Prison, Shrewsbury, also called by the prosecution, said the prisoner had been under his observation from 22nd February until 26th March. He thought that Taylor knew the nature of his act, and that it was wrong.

After the jury had taken just over 35 minutes to reach a 'Guilty' verdict, Mr Justice Byrne sentenced Taylor to death. Mr Davies immediately lodged an appeal, but on 22nd June the Home Secretary announced that he would not interfere with the due process of law. Accordingly, Milton Taylor was hanged at Walton Prison, Liverpool, on 29th June 1954.

TWO UNSOLVED MURDERS

The fact that a crime has not been solved does not, of course, mean that the police have closed the case. Far from it. There have been many murder cases where a conviction has been secured many years after the body was found – John Taft 'The Beauty in the Bath' murderer, for example, was arrested and convicted 16 years after the crime was committed, and, in July 2002, Wallasey man Thomas Bowman was sentenced to life imprisonment for murdering his wife 24 years previously.

The two unsolved murders described here are still very much current investigations, and an arrest could be made tomorrow, next week, next month, next year, or at some other time in the future. Or not at all. It must be emphasised that they are described as 'unsolved' because that was the case at the time of writing in 2002.

(A) Unanswered Questions in Winsford

It was the milk/bread roundsman who found Leslie Alan Gunthrip's body. He made the discovery on the morning of Thursday, 16th February 1978, when he made his daily call at the retired farmer's home, Bradford Mill Farm, Winsford. Because 72-year-old Gunthrip suffered with arthritis, he habitually left the door on the latch so that friends and those who had business with him could come and go without his having the discomfort of getting to his feet. On that particular morning, after the milkman had knocked and let himself in, as usual, he found Gunthrip sitting in his favourite armchair, dead.

At first the police thought that he had suffered a fatal heart attack, but a post-mortem revealed that he had died under a rain of blows from a blunt instrument of some sort, which had left him with a cerebral haemorrhage, cuts and a fractured skull.

Detective Chief Superintendent Gerry Williams of Cheshire Constabulary was appointed to lead the murder inquiry, and a team 130 officers was drafted in to assist him. Williams established a tentative theory that Gunthrip had surprised a burglar, and had been killed in the struggle which followed. It was not, however, a theory that was well supported by the facts. Nothing of value had been removed from the house, and the black tin box in which the farmer kept his housekeeping money was untouched. The only item known to have been taken was an ancient single-barrelled shotgun, which was so corroded that Williams issued a public warning that if anyone tried to fire the gun, it would explode.

Gunthrip was a well-known, respected and popular figure. He had particularly good relationships with the local schools, and was happy for them to conduct field study outings on his land; they, on their part, always invited him to school functions. Williams was able to dismiss the possibility of personal enmity at an early stage in his investigation.

Possibly, the police maintained the 'burglary' theory for lack of any other tenable motive. In fact, it seemed a particularly pointless murder at the time, and the 24 years which have passed since the body was found have yielded nothing that might make more sense of it.

The inquiry was launched with a flurry of activity. An underwater search team scoured 'Tommy's Hole', a fishing pool on Gunthrip's land, and a team, using dogs, quartered the banks of the nearby River Weaver, in an attempt to find the murder weapon. In the event, both exercises proved fruitless. Other officers began the painstaking, but essential, task of door-to-door questioning.

Winsford High Street in the 1970s – at the time of Leslie Gunthrip's murder.

On 2nd March the local *Middlewich Guardian* reported that, at about 7.30 pm on the evening of the murder, (here the reporter appears to have been guessing, but the pathologist's report to the inquest, held on 3rd March, stating that death had taken place at some time between 9 pm and 3 am revealed that he/she had been close to the truth) witnesses had seen two cars parked in Mill Lane, close to the farmhouse. One was a white hatchback, and the other was a red or orange saloon-type car. Others reported having seen a tramp in the area at the time concerned. They described him as having been between 40 and 50 years of age, about 5 feet 10 inches tall and having dark hair. The paper added that Chief Superintendent Williams was appealing for the drivers of the vehicles and the tramp to contact the police.

By the following issue of the paper, a week later, neither the drivers of the cars nor the tramp had come forward, but the possibility of another lead had emerged. It seemed that, on 2nd March, a girl aged about 14 had been overheard talking about the murder on a bus. She said that she had been intending to see Mr Gunthrip about a gun, when she heard that he had been killed. It seemed a very odd comment for a schoolgirl to make, and Williams appealed for her to contact the police.

The victim's relatives offered a reward of £1,000 to anyone who could furnish information leading to the arrest and conviction of the murderer.

According to the *Guardian*, by 6th March, more than 20,000 people had been interviewed in the course of the door-to-door operation. For all that, the police appeared to be making no progress. Neither the drivers of the cars nor the girl on the bus had come forward. A number of tramps had been interviewed, but none fitting the description given of the one spotted near the murder scene.

On 22nd March the paper's report on the crime bore the headline: POLICE 'STUMPED'.

On 6th April the paper reported that Williams had switched his inquiry headquarters from Winsford to Chester, and that he was commuting daily. In addition, the task force of officers had been reduced from 130 to 25.

By the following week, it seems, there was nothing new for the *Guardian* to report: the paper did not even mention the crime. By the end of the year, the police presence in Winsford had been reduced to normal levels.

And there the matter rests, for the moment. Until the murderer is arrested, there appears to be no possibility of even beginning to understand what appears to be a totally pointless crime.

(B) The Brenda Evans Case
Another unsolved and apparently pointless murder pitched the tiny agricultural village of Poulton onto the front pages

of the national newspapers. The victim, pretty 17-year-old blonde, Brenda Evans, of Yewtree Cottage, Poulton worked at the post office/general store in the neighbouring village of Pulford. Every working day lunchtime Brenda would walk the half mile to a meal with her uncle and aunt, Mr and Mrs Selwyn Davies, who lived in Poulton.

On 7th October 1977 Brenda left her relatives' house at 1.50 pm, with a cheerful 'Bye, bye. See you later,' as usual, to walk back to work. Her route followed Old Lane, a quiet road, densely wooded on both sides – a route that she had taken on many previous occasions.

On previous occasions, however, she had always arrived back at the post office in good time to start work when it reopened after the lunch break. Her non-appearance at her usual time on 7th October surprised the postmaster, Samuel Roberts. Half way through the afternoon her mother called at the shop. Immediately anxious at the news of her daughter's non-arrival, she checked with her sister, and when she discovered that Brenda had left her aunt's home at the usual time, her anxiety was displaced by alarm.

A number of friends and neighbours began a search of the area surrounding the route between the Selwyn Davies's home and the shop. They searched the woods and fields surrounding the two villages for four hours, before her fiancé's mother, 51-year-old Mrs Edith Pritchard, found her body.

'I don't know what made me go to the wood,' she said later. 'It was as if something was tugging inside me – forcing me to go there. I looked around, shouted for Brenda, and then went inside this old hut. Later, I looked down the manhole at the back of the building. I got down on my hands and knees, and I could see something blue with a little button on it. I leaned right in and saw Brenda. I tried to reach down and get her out. I just did not know what to do. I ran home and was crying and screaming every yard of the way.'

Police stand guard at the spot where the body of Brenda Evans was found in October 1977. (The Times)

Brenda had been strangled with her own tights, and dumped down the 12ft deep manhole – a mere 500 yards from a field where Brenda's fiancé, 20-year-old farm worker John Pritchard, had been cutting hedges that same afternoon.

Detective Chief Superintendent Gerry Williams was placed in charge of the investigation, supported by a team of 70 officers. They combed the surrounding area, and interviewed the members of a gang of workmen who had been laying new water mains in Old Lane on the day Brenda was murdered. Over the following days and weeks, they visited every house in Poulton and Pulford. They also stopped vehicles on the nearby Chester-to-Wrexham main road and questioned the drivers. In total they interviewed some 5,000 people and took some 1,000 statements. A reconstruction of Brenda's last walk was held in a bid to jog people's memories.

A local woman driver testified to passing along Old Lane and seeing Brenda. Seconds later, she saw a dark-blue Mk 2 Ford Cortina turn into Old Lane from the opposite direction and head towards the girl. Another witness saw a green Daf car turn out of Old Lane and onto the Chester-Wrexham road. Despite nationwide appeals neither driver contacted the police.

Convinced that they were looking for a local man, the police made a start with John Pritchard. They questioned him for a total of 27 hours, and they did not release him from police bail – without charge – for four weeks.

Two months on, just as the investigation had been scaled down, a new development brought fresh fear to the locals. Scratched into the paintwork of the telephone kiosk which stood close to the spot where Brenda's body was found was the chilling message, 'I will strike again'. Whether it really was the killer's work, or that of someone with a warped sense of humour, it was enough to jolt villagers out of their gradual readjustment. And the Brenda Evans murder hit the headlines again .

In January the police told the press that they had narrowed their list of suspects down to a handful of local men but, in the event, the leads all came to nothing.

Time moved on. Brenda's family left the area, and Poulton and Pulford residents settled down into their former peaceful obscurity.

Which is where the matter stands – for the moment.

BIBLIOGRAPHY

Bamforth, Peter *Cheshire Curiosities* (Dovecote Press, 1992)

Cheshire Sheaf (Various editions)

Head, Robert *Congleton, Past and Present* (1887) Old Vicarage Publications centenary edition (1987)

Latham, Frank *Alpraham – The History of a Village* (Family History Society of Cheshire, 1971)

Leatham, Richard *Notebook 1949–52* (unpublished)

Yarwood, Derek *Outrages – Fatal and Other. A Chronicle of Cheshire Crime 1612–1912* (Didsbury, 1991)

The author also consulted a wide variety of newspapers and magazines, including: *Cheshire Life*, the *Liverpool Daily Post* and *The Times*.